2

MR. ROOSEVELT'S FOUR FREEDOMS

MR. ROOSEVELT'S
FOUR FREEDOMS

THE STORY BEHIND THE
UNITED NATIONS CHARTER

By Frank Donovan

ILLUSTRATED

DODD, MEAD & COMPANY

NEW YORK

Library of Congress Catalog Card Number: 66-12040

Printed in the United States of America
by Vail-Ballou Press, Inc., Binghamton, N. Y.

Quotations from *The Memoirs of Cordell Hull* by Cordell Hull are reprinted with permission of the Macmillan Company. Copyright 1948 by Cordell Hull.

Quotations from *Where Are We Heading* and *Seven Decisions That Shaped History* by Sumner Welles, copyright by Sumner Welles, are reprinted by permission of Harper and Row, Publishers.

Quotations from *Calculated Risk* by Mark Clark is reprinted by permission of Harper and Row, Publishers.

Quotations from *The Private Papers of Senator Vandenberg* by Arthur Vandenberg are reprinted by permission of Houghton Mifflin Company.

Quotations from *The Grand Alliance, The Hinge of Fate* and *Closing the Ring* by Winston Churchill are reprinted by permission of Houghton, Mifflin Company.

Contents

Illustrations

MR. ROOSEVELT'S FOUR FREEDOMS

1

The Practical Idealist

I get everlastingly angry at those who assert vociferously that the Four Freedoms and the Atlantic Charter are nonsense because they are unattainable. If those people had lived a century and a half ago they would have sneered and said that the Declaration of Independence was utter piffle. If they had lived nearly a thousand years ago they would have laughed uproariously at the ideals of the Magna Carta. And if they had lived several thousand years ago they would have derided Moses when he came from the Mountain with the Ten Commandments.

So, in 1943, did Franklin Delano Roosevelt express his contempt for those who would become critics of the purposes of the United Nations Organization—which did not yet exist. And, in so doing, he related his ideals for a new world order to past milestones in human relations. The Declaration of Independence and the Magna Carta established the principle that the primary purpose of the state is to protect and advance man's human, God-given rights. The Ten Commandments contain the great moral code upon which a lasting civilization was based. These two things were the foundation stones on which, he believed, a new and better world could be built: the morality of states as well as individuals and a universal recognition of the dignity and the basic rights of every individual, everywhere.

Franklin Roosevelt's idealism was the spark which brought the United Nations Organization into being. Far more than any other man, he is responsible for the existence of this international body. He even seems to have coined the name "United Nations." Yet, paradoxically, he cared very little about the United Nations Organization, as such. This was machinery—and F.D.R. had little interest in machinery or methods. The machinery was largely built and the methods devised by others, from many lands. Roosevelt's concern was for objectives, not methods, and starting in the 1920's, his thinking slowly evolved a different concept of political, social, and economic international relations.

He did not expect that his ideals would quickly be realized merely by the establishment of an organization dedicated to them. Inspired by the Bok peace awards in 1923 he had written: "The world patient cannot be cured overnight by a simple surgical operation. A systematic course of treatment extending through the years will prove the only means of saving his life." What to him was important was that, first, certain basic principles be recognized, that they be interpreted into objectives and that a start be made toward realizing these objectives—slow step by slow step. That is all he hoped for from any international organization. He expressed his personal purpose when he said: "Somebody has to breathe heart and ideals on a large scale into this whole subject if it is to be put into effect on a world-wide basis."

Because Roosevelt's ideals are the basis of the goals of the United Nations Organization, it may be interesting to trace briefly their development through his long public career. First, it is necessary to recognize some of F.D.R.'s inate characteristics. Throughout his entire life he was a humanitarian. He was, from the time he entered public life, a vigorous reformer—a Roosevelt family trait. And he was, in later life, an idealist, but not a "head in the clouds" idealist of the Woodrow Wilson type. He was also a pragmatist, a practical realist. He dreamed his dreams, most of them great in scope, some of them Utopian, but in trying to effectuate them his feet were firmly on the ground.

This is one reason he has so often been accused by his critics of inconsistency. He was frequently inconsistent on the surface. After making a lofty statement of purpose he sometimes performed an act which seemed to be diametrically opposed. This did not mean that he had denied the purpose. The act was usually an expediency required by the practical concerns of the moment. As an instance, after firmly expressing his conviction that colonial peoples should be free to order their own lives, he sent word, during the war, to Marshal Pétain, head of the Vichy French Government, that one of his "greatest wishes is to see France reconstituted in the post-war period," and "the word 'France' in the mind of the President includes the French Colonial Empire." This was an obvious contradiction of his condemnation of colonialism—but the problem of the moment was to keep the Vichy French from cooperating with their German conquerors; specifically, to keep the French fleet out of German hands. To tell the French that German defeat meant the loss of their colonies was not the way to meet the immediate problem.

Another Roosevelt trait which guided the principles and purposes of the United Nations was his everlasting optimism. He believed that most people were inherently "good." He frequently voiced the theme that 90 percent of the world's people could be relied upon to live together in brotherly love if given the proper opportunity and leadership. And he believed that, with few and occasional exceptions, the governments of states could be lifted to the same high moral plane as the people; that they could learn to solve their problems by working peaceably together. This is the essence of the United Nations.

In the early years of his public life there was little evidence of the idealist in Roosevelt. In 1914, as Assistant Secretary of the Navy under Woodrow Wilson, he rather sneeringly said that Secretary of the Navy Josephus Daniels' extreme depression at the outbreak of World War I was due to the shock to his "faith in human nature and civilization and similar idealistic nonsense." He was also an ardent militarist, particularly a "big navy" man. During the early days of World War I he was so frustrated when his views went unheeded by the pacifistic Daniels and Wilson that he wrote his wife that the people should be told the truth about America's military weakness, "instead of a lot of soft mush about everlasting peace which so many statesmen are handing out to a gullible public." Until he came under the spell of Wilson's idealism he derided those who talked of world government as addlepated extremists and maintained that, for the foreseeable future, there would always be a need for strong military forces.

His conversion was almost comparable to that of Saul on the road to Damascus. He admitted this in 1919 when he said: "Last spring I thought the League of Nations merely a beautiful Utopial dream." In 1920, campaigning for Vice President with Wilson, he made some eight hundred speeches in defense of the League. And by the early 1920's he was a strong advocate of disarmament.

During most of Roosevelt's thirty-five years as a public figure he observed the collapse of an old order. Throughout most of the nineteenth century the Holy Alliance formed at the end of the Napoleonic Wars had, in the main, preserved peace in Europe. True, it had quickly degenerated into a "balance of power" concept in international relations that was far different than the idealistic scheme which Tsar Alexander had originally proposed. But the countries of Western Europe, and the United States, had prospered and progressed during the period. European countries were busy building empires in Asia and Africa —assuming "the white man's burden" of colonialism which, in those days, was considered praiseworthy rather than reprehensible. As a result of this same Holy Alliance, President James Monroe made the speech that became the bible of United States foreign policy—the Monroe Doctrine, which proclaimed isolationism for the Western Hemisphere.

World War I highlighted the disintegration of the old system, and in the years between wars, Roosevelt expressed varied reasons for its collapse and started to form opinions on which he would base his concept of a new world order. He believed that the peace with Germany had been too "soft" because it permitted the continuance of a militaristic philosophy. He was convinced that the League of Nations could have been a moral force for organizing world opinion on the side of peace, law, and order, but that it was doomed to failure because the United States, one of the world's great powers, did not participate.

During the early 1920's Roosevelt became convinced that the League was degenerating into a new Holy Alliance of power politics and, in 1923, proposed that it be scrapped in favor of a different international organization which he called the "Society of Nations." In many ways this was the League warmed over with some controversial aspects eliminated to make it acceptable to the U.S. Senate. This was an example of his concern with objectives rather than methods. The goal of the League was good, but the machinery was not working. To Roosevelt it was obvious that the thing to do was try some other road to the same goal—not to give up the objective.

Another cause for the breakdown of the old system was, in Roosevelt's opinion, the rise of economic nationalism. He was never an outright "free trader," but he believed that the high tariffs favored by his political opponents had such a frustrating adverse effect on the economies of other countries that they were a threat to peace. He was convinced that economic cooperation rather than economic isolation was essential to world progress and was distressed at the mad scramble of many countries to become economically self-sufficient regardless of what this policy meant to other members of the family of nations.

A favorite theme of F.D.R.'s was that governments throughout the world were not facing up to twentieth-century problems and responsibilities. As a reformer, he believed that the leadership of the state should foster progress in the interests of what he called social justice. By this he meant, among other things, universal access to education, better job opportunities and working conditions, social security, government concern for health and nutrition, and other measures which were then considered radical. He traced the rise of communism and the fascist dictators to the failure of governments with old-fashioned concepts which did not meet new responsibilities.

Another cause for the complete collapse of the old system, in Roosevelt's mind, was the armament race which started after the breakdown of disarmament measures in the 1920's. Not only would nations be tempted to play with their new toys, once they had them, but the cost of arms was depriving the people of butter and creating dissatisfaction and tensity which could breed war. This was particularly true, he believed, of small nations which could least afford a competition in armaments and whose possession of weapons might lead to little wars which would grow into big wars.

Imperialism was another cause for world tensions in the twentieth century, in Roosevelt's mind. On this subject he also underwent a conversion from his pre-World War I thinking. In his younger years F.D.R. was himself something of a humanitarian imperialist along the lines of his cousin Theodore. He believed that it was necessary for the United States to dominate the Caribbean, by force if necessary. He thought that one of the finest things that ever happened was the intervention of U.S. Marines in Haiti. Not only was this necessary for the security of the United States, but it was good for the Haitians. He was not an imperialist in the sense of exploiting other peoples; but he saw nothing wrong in a strong power imposing on a weak neighbor the benefits of its superior political and moral system to bring about better "social justice" for the people. If this had to be done with Marines, the means justified the end.

From this position, during the 1920's and increasingly in the next decade, Roosevelt veered to the belief that all forms of imperialism were basically wrong. Colonialism and spheres of influence almost invariably led to the exploitation of one group of people by another. As his idealism grew he became convinced that this was basically evil and completely out of step with the new world order as he envisioned it.

Added to all these basic causes for the collapse of the old order—and brought into being by them—there were, in the 1930's, a particular group whom Roosevelt considered "Bad Guys." The immoral 10 percent that he mentioned were favored by the times. Leading the parade of villains were Hitler's Nazis, Mussolini's Fascists, and the Japanese War Lords. In the procession were the weak appeasers who were afraid to oppose them, the arch-conservatives who resisted change, the "merchants of death" who put profits before peace, and selfish economic royalists in general.

When Roosevelt came to the White House in 1933 he had in mind that something should be done to replace the old system of international relationships and that the United States should take the leadership in doing it. On this he stood almost alone. The United States had lived with isolationism until World War I and had decisively rejected membership in an international organization after the war, to become more strongly isolationist during the 1920's and 1930's. Roosevelt was one of the very few who realized, as early as the teen years, that isolationism was no longer feasible. He was amazed, in 1914, that nobody else in the Navy Department seemed to feel that the outbreak of war in Europe had any direct bearing on the welfare of the United States.

Roosevelt's domestic economic theories may be—and have been—criticized; there are those who condemn his ideas on a strong, paternalistic government, and he sometimes perverted history to his own ends. But none can quarrel with his concept of twentieth-century geopolitics. "He was one of the first to realize that all wars are potentially global wars—that the states of the modern world are so interdependent that any unrest anywhere has potential meaning everywhere." For years he tried patiently to teach that isolationism was not only futile but impossible. Not only had the nature of war changed so that broad oceans were no longer defensive barriers; but all nations depend so on international trade that no nation can be economically self-sufficient. Regardless of humanitarian ideals, from a purely practical standpoint the United States had to participate in world affairs; and morally, politically, financially, and technologically he believed that his country was in a position which required it to take the leadership.

When F.D.R. assumed the Presidency he had to move slowly in this area. As a realist he accepted the fact that expediency, in terms of the depression, required a brief period of economic nationalism to put out the fire at home. Isolationist public opinion would not accept any progressive ideas on internationalism. And his Secretary of State, Cordell Hull, while agreeing with the President on many of his basic theories, was extremely cautious about disturbing the *status quo*. However, Roosevelt did, in his first inaugural address, express the underlying theme of his new concept of international relations. He said that he would "dedicate this nation to the policy of the good neighbor—the neighbor who resolutely respects himself, and because he does so, respects the rights of others—the neighbor who respects the sanctity of his agreements in and with a world of good neighbors."

At the time, not much attention was paid to this. Six weeks later Roosevelt expanded on the good neighbor theme in a speech to the Pan-American Union in which he said:

Friendship among nations, as among individuals, calls for constructive efforts to muster the forces of humanity in order that an atmosphere of close understanding and cooperation may be cultivated. It involves mutual obligations and responsibilities, for it is only by sympathetic respect for the rights of others and a scrupulous fulfillment of the corresponding obligations by each member of the community that a true fraternity can be maintained.

The essential qualities of a true Pan-Americanism must be the same as those which constitute a good neighbor, namely, mutual understanding and, through such understanding, a sympathetic appreciation of the other's point of view. It is only in this manner that we can hope to build up a system of which confidence, friendship, and good-will are the cornerstones. . . .

Your Americanism and mine must be a structure built of confidence, cemented by a sympathy which recognizes only equality and fraternity. It finds its source and being in the hearts of men and dwells in the temple of the intellect.

From this the "Good Neighbor" policy became associated in the minds of most people with United States–Latin American relationships. But Roosevelt originally applied it to "a world of good neighbors," and when he talked of confidence, sympathy, equality, and fraternity he had in mind the neighbors of the world as well as the neighbors of the Western Hemisphere.

International relations in the Western Hemisphere reached an all-time low during the early years of the twentieth century as a result of President Theodore Roosevelt's policy of the "big stick" and the "dollar diplomacy" which flowered under President Taft. F.D.R.'s predecessors in the White House, from Wilson to Hoover, had endeavored to make some improvements, but when Roosevelt took office "Yankee" was a term of supreme contempt in Latin America and "Monroe Doctrine" were fighting words.

For over a century the attitude of the United States toward its southern neighbors had been one of hegemony for the Colossus of the North. The Monroe Doctrine was a policy to assure hemisphere security which would be applied unilaterally by the United States when and as it saw fit, without regard for the attitude or opinions of the other American states. The Good Neighbor policy changed this by inviting the southern countries to confer as equals. The United States renounced the right of intervention and proposed that all matters of interhemisphere relationships be settled by mutual rather than unilateral decisions. This ultimately led to the Organization of American States.

By the latter 1930's international relationships in the Western Hemisphere had improved to a point that Roosevelt could point to the Good Neighbor policy as a basis of a new world order. He pointed out:

The 300,000,000 citizens in the American republics are not different from other human beings. We have the same problems, the same differences, even the same material for controversy, which exist elsewhere. . . . There are not wanting here all the usual rivalries, all the normal human desires for power and expansion, all of the commercial problems.

There were in the Americas, as in the Old World, he said, "diversities of race, of language, of custom, of natural resources; and of intellectual forces at least as great as those which prevailed in Europe." The difference was, he pointed out, "a new, and powerful idea—that of the community of nations." And he added, "if that process can be successful here, is it too much to hope that a similar intellectual and spiritual process may succeed elsewhere?"

A month after he originally enunciated his Good Neighbor theory in 1933, Roosevelt addressed a plea to the heads of fifty-four nations to cooperate in the Disarmament Conference which was then in session at Geneva and the World Economic Conference which was about to meet in London. The recipients ranged, alphabetically, from Albania's King Zog I to Yugoslavia's King Alexander I. To this august group the President said:

The happiness, the prosperity, and the very lives of the men, women and children who inhabit the whole world are bound up in the decisions which their governments will make in the near future. The improvement of social conditions, the preservation of individual human rights, and the furtherance of social justice are dependent upon these decisions.

The World Economic Conference will meet soon and must come to the conclusions quickly. The world cannot await deliberations long drawn out. The conference must establish order in place of the present chaos by a stabilization of currencies, by freeing the flow of world trade, and by international action to raise price levels. It must, in short, supplement individual domestic programs for economic recovery by wise and considered international action.

The Disarmament Conference has labored for more than a

year and, as yet, has been unable to reach satisfactory conclusions. Confused purposes still clash dangerously. Our duty lies in the direction of bringing practical results through concerted action based upon the greatest good to the greatest number. Before the imperative call of this great duty, petty obstacles must be swept away and petty aims forgotten. A selfish victory is always destined to be an ultimate defeat. The furtherance of durable peace for our generation in every part of the world is the only goal worthy of our best efforts.

All of the heads of state who replied endorsed Roosevelt's point of view. Nobody did anything. Later Roosevelt would ruefully say:

We have sought steadfastly to assist international movements to prevent war. We cooperated to the bitter end—and it was a bitter end—in the work of the General Disarmament Conference. When it failed we sought a separate treaty to deal with the manufacture of arms and the international traffic in arms. That proposal also came to nothing. We participated—again to the bitter end—in a conference to continue naval limitations.

In the latter part of the speech from which the preceding is quoted, as in many messages and addresses, Roosevelt subtly sought, through the 1930's, to combat the conviction of Americans that security lay in isolationism. On this occasion he said:

We shun political commitments which might entangle us in foreign wars; we avoid connection with the political activities of the League of Nations; but I am glad to say that we have cooperated whole-heartedly in the social and humanitarian work at Geneva. Thus we are a part of the world effort to control traffic in narcotics, to improve international health, to help child welfare, to eliminate double taxation, and to better working conditions and laboring hours throughout the world.

We are not isolationist except in so far as we seek to isolate ourselves completely from war. Yet we must remember that so long as war exists on earth there will be some danger that even the nation which most ardently desires peace may be drawn into war.

During his first two terms F.D.R. made little progress in convincing the people or the Congress that the United States must accept responsibilities in the family of nations. In 1935 he pleaded with the Senate to approve United States participation in the International Court of Justice. The Senate said "No." When, in 1937, Japan invaded North China, the President made his famous "Quarantine Speech," designed perhaps as a trial balloon to test public opinion in the United States toward taking a stronger stand on such threatening international developments. He said:

There is a solidarity and interdependence about the modern world, both technically and morally, which makes it impossible for any nation completely to isolate itself from economic and political upheavals in the rest of the world, especially when such upheavals appear to be spreading and not declining. There can be no stability or peace either within nations or between nations except under laws and moral standards adhered to by all. International anarchy destroys every foundation for peace. It jeopardizes either the immediate or the future security of every nation, large or small. It is, therefore, a matter of interest and concern to the people of the United States that the sanctity of international treaties and the maintenance of international morality be restored. . . .

If we are to have a world in which we can breathe freely and live in amity without fear . . . The peace-loving nations must make a concerted effort in opposition to those violations of treaties and those ignorings of humane instinct which today are creating a state of international anarchy and instability from which there is no escape through mere isolation of neutrality. . . .

It seems to be unfortuntely true that the epidemic of world lawlessness is spreading. When an epidemic of physical disease starts to spread, the community approves and joins in a quarantine of the patients in order to protect the health of the community against the spread of the disease.

If F.D.R. was seeking to test public opinion with this speech he got a quick reaction—a violently hostile one. The American people had no interest in joining the world community to quarantine international lawlessness.

In the late 1930's, as the Japanese swept through China, as the Italian Fascists conquered Albania, as Hitler gobbled up Austria and dismembered Czechoslovakia, most Americans were concerned solely with neutrality. Roosevelt, advocate of disarmament, now pleaded for money for arms for defense. In his annual message in 1939 he told the Congress:

There comes a time in the affairs of men when they must prepare to defend not their homes alone but the tenets of faith and humanity on which their churches, their governments and their very civilization are founded. The defense of religion, democracy and of good faith among nations is all the same fight. To save one we must now make up our minds to save all. . . .

The world has grown so small and weapons of attack so swift that no nation can be safe in its will to peace so long as any other single powerful nation refuses to settle its grievances at the council table. For if any government bristling with implements of war insists on policies of force, weapons of defense give the only safety.

He ended this message emotionally by saying:

Once I prophesied that this generation of Americans had a rendezvous with destiny. That prophecy comes true. To us much is given; more is expected. This generation will "nobly save or meanly lose the last best hope of earth . . . The way is plain, peaceful, generous, just—a way which, if followed, the world will forever applaud and God must forever bless."

As Hitler and Mussolini continued to rattle their sabers more loudly during the spring of 1939, Roosevelt requested assurance from the dictators that they would not attack or invade neighboring states and offered to act as a "friendly intermediary" in conveying such assurance to other nations and securing reciprocal assurances from them. He proposed that, after such assurances were exchanged:

Two essential problems shall promptly be discussed in the resulting peaceful surroundings, and in those discussions the Government of the United States will gladly take part.

The discussions which I have in mind relate to the most effective and immediate manner through which the peoples of the world can obtain progressive relief from the crushing burden of armament which is each day bringing them more closely to the brink of disaster. Simultaneously the Government of the United States would be prepared to take part in discussions looking toward the most practical manner of opening up avenues of international trade to the end that every nation of the earth may be enabled to buy and sell on equal terms in the world market as well as to possess assurance of obtaining the materials and products of peaceful economic life. At the same time, those governments other than the United States which are directly interested could undertake such political discussions as they may consider necessary or desirable.

To justify this mild offer of international cooperation to isolationist America, Roosevelt hastened to assure the people that he had offered to act as a "friendly intermediary," not a mediator, and had specifically excluded the United States from political discussions. He pointed out that his proposed discussions of disarmament and economic affairs represented "nothing, absolutely nothing, new that we have not been doing right along."

After European war became a reality in the fall of 1939, F.D.R. penned a plea for cooperation in the interests of peace in a Christmas message to Pope Pius XII, with similar letters to the presidents of the Federal Council of Churches and the Jewish Theological Seminary of America. Although his messages were addressed to religious leaders, his appeal was to men of good faith everywhere. He wrote:

The world has created for itself a civilization capable of giving to mankind security and peace firmly set in the foundations of religious teachings. Yet, though it has conquered the earth, the sea, and even the air, civilization today passes through war and travail.

I take heart in remembering that in a similar time, Isaiah first prophesied the birth of Christ. Then, several centuries before His coming, the condition of the world was not unlike that which we see today. Then, as now, a conflagration had been set; and nations walked dangerously in the light of the fires they had themselves kindled. But in that very moment a spiritual rebirth was foreseen. . . . There was promised a new age wherein through renewed faith the upward progress of the human race would become more secure. . . .

I believe that while statesmen are considering a new order of things, the new order may well be at hand. I believe that it is even now being built, silently but inevitably, in the hearts of masses whose voices are not heard, but whose common faith will write the final history of our time. They know that unless there is belief in some guiding principle and some trust in a divine plan, nations are without light, and peoples perish. They know that the civilization handed down to us by our fathers was built by men and women who knew in their hearts that all were brothers because they were children of God. They believe that by His will enmities can be healed; that in His mercy the weak can find deliverance, and the strong can find grace in helping the weak.

In the grief and terror of the hour, these quiet voices, if they can be heard, may yet tell of the rebuilding of the world.

It is well that the world should think of this at Christmas.

Because the people of this nation have come to a realization that time and distance no longer exist in the older sense, they understand that that which harms one segment of humanity harms all the rest. They know that only by friendly association among the seekers of light and the seekers of peace everywhere can the forces of evil be overcome. . . .

It is my thought, therefore, that though no given action or given time may now be prophesied, it is well that we encourage a closer association between those in every part of the world—those in religion and those in government—who have a common purpose.

During 1940 most of Roosevelt's public utterances had to do with the immediate situation rather than long-range objectives. These included a continuing step-up in defense measures, repeated assurances that the United States would remain neutral, and requests to the Congress for legislation that would permit the United States to aid the opponents of the aggressors, short of war—specifically, a revision of the 1935 neutrality act which would permit this country to sell arms to belligerents on a cash-and-carry basis. From a practical standpoint this meant aid to Great Britain, the only belligerent with the maritime tonnage to "carry."

And the President struck out more boldly against isolationism. He used the occasion of Italy's declaration of war on France in June, 1940, to make his famous "Dagger in the Back" speech, in which he said:

Perception of danger, danger to our institutions, may come slowly or it may come with a rush and a shock as it has to the people of the United States in the past few months. This perception of danger, danger in a world-wide area—it has come to us clearly and overwhelmingly—we perceive the peril in a world-wide arena, an arena that may become so narrowed that only the Americas will retain the ancient faiths.

Some indeed still hold to the now somewhat obvious delusion that we of the United States can safely permit the United States to become a lone island, a lone island in a world dominated by the philosophy of force.

Such an island may be the dream of those who still talk and vote as isolationists. Such an island represents to me and to the overwhelming majority of Americans today a helpless nightmare, the helpless nightmare of a people without freedom; yes, the nightmare of a people lodged in prison, handcuffed, hungry, and fed through the bars from day to day by the contemptuous, unpitying masters of other continents.

Privately the U.S. State Department, under Roosevelt's and Hull's direction, was already thinking of America's participation in the peace—whenever it might come. Early in 1940 Secretary of State Hull said quietly that it would be essential in America's "own best interests" to apply to the peace, when it came, "the weight of our country's moral and material influence in creating a stable and enduring order under law." Privately, the Secretary declared that this "obviously meant a world organization."

Such talk was much too radical for public opinion at the time, but the State Department started to explore steps which might be taken to promote a lasting peaceful world order. During the so-called cold war in the early months of 1940, when Hitler paused after conquering Poland, the State Department invited a list of neutral nations to exchange views on "two basic problems connected with the establishment of a sound foundation for a lasting world peace; namely the establishment of the basis of a sound international economic system, and the limitation and reduction of armaments."

The German blitzkrieg conquest of Belgium, the Netherlands, and France and the isolation of Great Britain stymied this proposed conference of neutrals. But in preparation for it the U.S. State Department prepared a memorandum on postwar economic relations which became the basis of some of the thinking that would ultimately guide the United Nations in this area. It pointed out that there could be no lasting peace unless prewar economic policies were corrected. All countries must have greater economic opportunities in order to increase standards of living. This meant the removal of excessive tariffs, international agreement on the handling of foods and other essential commodities, and financial agreements to restore stable currencies and international credit. All this would obviously require some intergovernmental agencies, at least in the areas of commerce and finance.

In view of the war situation no complete memorandum on disarmament was prepared, but an exploratory note acknowledged that to achieve disarmament "and a force to make it effective . . . some machinery for political decision must exist." This statement forecast the abandonment of the long-held American policy of "no entangling alliances."

At this time Roosevelt also developed the principle of

"international trusteeship," which he would come to regard with increasing enthusiasm and seek to apply on a world-wide basis. This was originally exposed at a Pan-American Conference in Havana in July, 1940. There was danger that Germany might try to take over the possessions of France and the Netherlands in the Western Hemisphere. The United States proposed that, in the event of such action, the areas involved should be placed under "collective trusteeship" until their ultimate destiny was decided. This led to the establishment of an Inter-American Commission for Territorial Administration within the Pan-American Union.

At various times Roosevelt spoke of applying this principle of international trusteeship to several specific areas around the world. He thought that it should replace the old system of mandates which the League of Nations had applied to German colonies after World War I, because when a territory was mandated to a single country, that country usually came to feel that it had sovereignty over the territory.

Some of the areas for which Roosevelt mentioned international trusteeship after the war were Indochina, Malaya, the Dutch East Indies, and Korea. The latter, he thought, might be administered by a trusteeship consisting of the U.S.S.R., the United States, and China for twenty or thirty years until it was ready for independence. He also believed that international trusteeship was the answer for Palestine, with trustees representing all three religions that had an interest in this area: Christians, Moslems, and Jews. Thinking of the postwar refugee problem he at one time suggested that the Guianas be sequestered as a refugee settlement and wrote his wife that he was "considering the broad thought of creating a form of Pan-American trusteeship for situations of this kind. It is a new idea in international or Pan-American relationships but it is worth studying."

In view of what happened later, it is interesting that he mentioned most of the trouble spots of the 1950's and 1960's as areas where trusteeship rather than immediate independence should be applied.

A favorite theme of F.D.R.'s in relation to colonialism and trusteeship was the relationship of the United States and the Philippines, to whom, in 1936, a promise was made of future complete independence after a period of careful preparation for self-government and economic stability. Although he was opposed to colonialism and looked forward to a time when it would no longer exist, he was too much of a realist to hope that people who had long been dependent on the rule of a strong power could be expected to become stable independent states immediately.

The form of government under which colonial peoples or the inhabitants of the conquered countries of Europe would ultimately live must be decided, thought Roosevelt, by self-determination. For most colonial peoples this would take place after years of international trusteeship. For the people of Europe who were more advanced politically and economically it might happen after a short cooling-down period at the end of the war. Then plebiscites might settle such thorny questions as the relations of the Serbs, Croatians, and Slovenians in Yugoslavia, the Germans in the Sudeten area of Czechoslovakia, the boundaries of Poland, and the ultimate fate of the Lithuanians, Estonians, and Latvians who had been gobbled up by Russia.

On this thinking he received support from the people of

the United States, who assumed that self-determination meant democracy—they could not imagine any people voluntarily choosing any other form of government. But when F.D.R. came to bargain with the leaders of the other great powers he was opposed on this point more than any other. Winston Churchill was willing to go along with self-determination in Europe, but he was a confirmed colonialist who said: "I have not become the King's First Minister in order to preside over the liquidation of the British Empire." Joseph Stalin would not even discuss self-determination in the areas which Russia had taken over before she went to war.

Roosevelt's annual message to Congress on January 6, 1941, was his famous "Four Freedoms" speech in which he defined his goals for the postwar world. Most of this speech was devoted to the need for increased production for defense and a request for legislation that would permit the United States to provide arms for nations fighting aggression who no longer had cash with which to pay for them—a request which resulted in the Lend-Lease Act.

During World War I the United States had loaned vast sums to the Allies to purchase arms, with the understanding that the loans would be repaid after the war. No nation ever paid its debt except Finland. Recognizing that repayment in money would be impossible for war-torn nations, the Lend-Lease Act provided that repayment after World War II would be on some terms acceptable to the President, not necessarily cash.

Roosevelt was already thinking of using Lend-Lease to guide the postwar world economically and tied the Lend-Lease agreement with Great Britain to the Atlantic Charter. The agreement stipulated:

In the final determination of benefits to be provided to the United States of America by the Government of the United Kingdom in return for aid furnished . . . the terms and conditions thereof shall be such as not to burden commerce between the two countries but to promote mutually advantageous economic relations between them and the betterment of world-wide economic relations. To that end they shall include provision for agreed action by the United States of America and the United Kingdom, open to participation by all other countries of like mind, directed to the expansion by appropriate international and domestic measures, of production, employment, and the exchange and consumption of goods, which are the material foundations of the liberty and welfare of all peoples; to the elimination of all forms of discriminatory treatment in international commerce, and to the reduction of tariffs and other trade barriers; and, in general, to the attainment of all the economic objectives set forth in the Joint Declaration made on August 12, 1941, by the President of the United States of America and the Prime Minister of the United Kingdom.

A similar clause was contained in the Lend-Lease agreements with all other nations.

Even at this late date—exactly eleven months before the United States was drawn into the shooting war by the Japanese attack on Pearl Harbor—Roosevelt still found it necessary to hammer home to Americans that what was happening elsewhere in the world was of concern to the United States. In his Four Freedoms speech he said; "Therefore, as your President, performing my constitutional duty to 'give to the Congress information on the state of the Union' I find it necessary to report that the future and the safety of our country and of our democracy are overwhelmingly involved in events far beyond our borders." Further, he insisted that America must be concerned in victory for the democracies, for, he said:

No realistic American can expect from a dictator's peace international generosity, or return of true independence, or world disarmament, or freedom of expression, or freedom of religion—or even good business. Such a peace would bring no security for us or for our neighbors. Those, who would give up essential liberty to purchase a little temporary safety, deserve neither liberty nor safety. As a nation we may take pride in the fact that we are soft-hearted; but we cannot afford to be soft-headed.

The peace which Roosevelt sought could not be bought with other people's freedom. On the contrary, he declared:

. . . world order which we seek is the cooperation of free countries, working together in a friendly, civilized society. . . . In the future days, which we seek to make secure, we look forward to a world founded upon four essential human freedoms.

The first is freedom of speech and expression—everywhere in the world.

The second is freedom of every person to worship God in his own way—everywhere in the world.

The third is freedom from want—which, translated into world terms, means economic understandings which will secure to every nation a healthy peacetime life for its inhabitants—everywhere in the world.

The fourth is freedom from fear—which, translated into world terms, means a world-wide reduction of armaments to such a point and in such a thorough fashion that no nation will be in position to commit an act of physical aggression against any neighbor—anywhere in the world.

That is no vision of a distant millennium. It is a definite basis for a kind of world attainable in our own time and generation. . . .

This nation has placed its destiny in the hands and heads and hearts of its millions of free men and women; and its faith in freedom under the guidance of God. Freedom means the supremacy of human rights everywhere. Our support goes to those who struggle to gain those rights or keep them.

Although in the speech itself he said that the world of freedom he described was not a "vision of a distant millennium" but was "attainable in our own . . . generation," F.D.R. made several other statements which indicated that he envisioned universal freedom as a goal toward which humanity must strive, rather than a new order which could be achieved in the near future. He generally talked more of making "steady progress" toward the Four Freedoms than of their immediate attainment. But he maintained that these freedoms were as essential to man as "air and sunlight, bread and salt. Deprive him of these freedoms and he dies—deprive him of part of them and a part of him withers. Give them to him in full and abundant measure and he will cross the threshold of a new age, the greatest age of man."

2

The Atlantic Charter

One afternoon in late July, Harry Hopkins came into the garden of Downing Street and we sat together in the sunshine. Presently he said that the President would like very much to have a meeting with me in some lonely bay or other. I replied at once that I was sure the Cabinet would give me leave. Thus all was soon arranged. Placentia Bay, in Newfoundland, was chosen, the date of August 9 [1941] was fixed, and our latest battleship, the *Prince of Wales,* was placed under orders accordingly. I had the keenest desire to meet Mr. Roosevelt, with whom I had now corresponded with increasing intimacy for nearly two years.

So wrote British Prime Minister Winston Churchill to describe briefly the background for the dramatic first meeting between the leaders of the two English-speaking nations. Both great showmen, they took delight in holding their first conference secretly aboard battleships anchored in a remote bay off the coast of Newfoundland. Churchill

27

left London quietly with his retinue, boarded his battleship, and disappeared. Roosevelt embellished his play-acting by publicly announcing that he was going on a fishing trip aboard the Presidential yacht *Potomac*. Because he wanted complete rest, no press representatives were to be included in the party. At sea, he transshipped to the cruiser *Augusta* and, with a small flotilla, steamed to the rendezvous to await Churchill.

Several participants have described the meeting. They all agree on the dinners that were exchanged in the captain's salons of the two flagships; on the Scotch grouse which Churchill brought to feast the Americans; on the nineteen hundred and fifty gift boxes containing fruit, cheese, and cigarettes which Roosevelt brought for the British crew; on the solemn and impressive Anglo-American worship service which was held on the deck of the *Prince of Wales*. On much else the accounts do not agree.

It is certain that Churchill's principal hope for the conference was to get a commitment from Roosevelt that the United States would enter the war. The President's son, Elliott, who was present, quotes the Prime Minister as saying, at the first dinner, "It's your only chance. You've *got* to come in beside us! If you don't declare war, declare war, I say, without waiting for them to strike the first blow, they'll strike it after we've gone under, and their first blow will be their last as well."

Another matter for concern to Churchill was Roosevelt's attitude toward Russia, which had been invaded by Germany less than seven weeks before the meeting. Elliott quoted a conversation that he had with his father in which the President said, of the British, "They'll be worried

about how much of our production we're going to divert
to the Russians."

"And?"

"I know already how much faith the P.M. has in Russia's ability to stay in the war." He snapped his fingers to
indicate zero.

"I take it you have more faith than that."

"Harry Hopkins has more. He's able to convince me."

Elliott Roosevelt is not generally considered as a good
objective reporter, and the dialogue he recorded in his
book—published five years after the event—is probably the
product of imagination rather than memory. But the
points of view reflected seem to be valid. Harry Hopkins
was an ex-social worker who had been associated with
Roosevelt since the latter was governor of New York. By
1941, and increasingly during the war years, he was virtually the President's alter ego in some aspects of foreign relations. He had come to the Atlantic meeting directly from a
visit to Joseph Stalin in Moscow. The Russian leader seems
to have mesmerized him to the point that he was completely "sold" on the Russian ability to combat the
Germans—in which he proved to be right—and on the Russian honesty of purpose in seeking the same goals as the
democracies—in which he was woefully wrong.

Russia had a mutual nonaggression treaty with Germany
which Hitler broke on June 22, 1941, when he invaded the
Communist state. Prior to that date Russia had released a
continuous tirade of condemnation against the "decadent
democracies," England and the United States. Despite this,
Churchill had gone on the air on the day of the invasion to
proclaim British support for Russia, saying:

. . . we shall give whatever help we can to Russia and the Russian people. We shall appeal to all our friends and allies in every part of the world to take the same course and pursue it, as we shall faithfully and steadfastly to the end. . . .

The Russian danger is, therefore, our danger, and the danger of the United States, just as the cause of any Russian fighting for his hearth and home is the cause of free men and free peoples in every quarter of the globe.

However, Churchill never had real faith in Russian performance or promises. Roosevelt had either faith or hope. This difference would be an important factor in the negotiations which led to a postwar international organization.

Perhaps the most reliable accounts of the significant events of the Atlantic meeting were written, on the American side, by Under Secretary of State Sumner Welles in his book *Where Are We Heading?*, and on the British side by Winston Churchill in the third volume of his World War II memoirs, *The Grand Alliance*. Sumner Welles reported on what Roosevelt hoped for from the meeting by writing:

President Roosevelt, before he had left Washington for the Atlantic meeting, had told me in some detail how he thought the approaching meeting with the British Prime Minister should be utilized to hold out hope to the enslaved peoples of the world. The English-speaking democracies both stood for principles of freedom and of justice. They should jointly bind themselves now to establish at the conclusion of the war a new world order based upon these principles.

Churchill confirmed this by writing:

President Roosevelt told me at one of our first conversations that he thought it would be well if we could draw up a joint declaration laying down certain broad principles which should guide our policies along the same road. Wishing to follow up this most helpful suggestion, I gave him the next day . . . a tentative outline of such a declaration.

The Prime Minister's initial draft contained five points:

First, their countries seek no aggrandisement, territorial or other.

Second, they desire to see no territorial changes that do not accord with the freely expressed wishes of the peoples concerned.

Third, they respect the right of all peoples to choose the form of government under which they will live. They are only concerned to defend the rights of freedom of speech and thought, without which such choice must be illusory.

Fourth, they will strive to bring about a fair and equitable distribution of essential produce, not only within their territorial boundaries, but between the nations of the world.

Fifth, they seek a peace which will not only cast down forever the Nazi tyranny, but by effective international organization will afford to all States and peoples the means of dwelling in security within their own bounds and of traversing the seas and oceans without fear of lawless assault or the need of maintaining burdensome armaments.

Churchill added in his memoirs: "Considering all the tales of my reactionary, Old-World outlook, and the pain this is said to have caused the President, I am glad it should be on the record that the substance and spirit of what came to be called the Atlantic Charter was in its first draft a British production cast in my own words."

Churchill's draft of the charter was revised by Sumner Welles, and this draft was again revised by F.D.R. Two pages of this second draft are reproduced in this volume, showing the President's handwritten changes.

The revision in point three, dealing with self-determination, is negligible. Welles removed the reference to defending "the rights of free speech and thought." He later explained this change by saying: "It was . . . more than doubtful that the American Congress would at that moment have approved a pledge by the government of the United States to 'defend the rights of freedom of speech and thought' when those rights were abrogated in every Axis country." Roosevelt added, with an eye toward public opinion and morale in the conquered countries, "and they hope that self-government may be restored to those from whom it has forcibly been removed."

Points four and five caused the most difficulty. Welles wrote: "The assurances proposed by Article 4 [in the Churchill draft] . . . meant precisely nothing. They were reminiscent of the pious hopes expressed in a thousand and one economic conferences that 'a fair and equitable international distribution of commodities' would come into being, during the very years when tariffs were being built up." He redrafted the point to read: "Fourth, they will endeavor to further the enjoyment by all peoples of access on equal terms to the markets and to the raw materials which are needed for their economic prosperity." Roosevelt changed this to read "access without discrimination and on equal terms."

Churchill pointed out that he could not sign a document containing the words "without discrimination and on equal terms" without submitting it to the Dominion governments. It violated the Ottawa Convention of 1932 which established the principle of Imperial Preference within the British Commonwealth. Because the delay in getting approval from the Dominions would make it impossible to release the document at the end of the conference, Roosevelt agreed to eliminate the objectionable words, but he wanted the thought expressed that the vanquished Germans and Italians would have postwar economic opportunities. They finally compromised on a point four which read: "Fourth, they will endeavor, with due respect for their existing obligations, to further the enjoyment by all states, great or small, victor or vanquished, of access, on equal terms, to the trade and to the raw materials of the world which are needed for their economic prosperity."

The most difficult area of compromise was Churchill's fifth point. His casual reference to "burdensome armaments" was not nearly strong enough to please Roosevelt. The President wanted disarmament spelled out in detail. He wrote out in longhand what was, in this draft, a sixth point:

"Sixth, because the future of peace is impossible if armament by land, sea and air continues in the hands of any nation which threatens to use force outside its frontiers we believe that disarmament of such nations is essential. We say this in the hope that the whole world may be guided in spirit to the goal of abandonment of force."

On the other hand, F.D.R. would not agree to the words "effective international organization," which he crossed out in Welles' draft. Both Churchill and Welles pressed F.D.R. on this and the Under Secretary later wrote:

The President replied that he did not feel that he could agree to this because of the suspicions and opposition that such a statement on his part would create in the United States. He said that he himself would not be in favor of the creation of a new Assembly of the League of Nations, at least until after a period of time had passed and during which international police force composed of the United States and Great Britain had had an opportunity of functioning. Mr. Churchill said that he did not feel that he would be candid if he did not express to the President his feeling that [this] point would create a great deal of opposition from the extreme internationalists. The President replied that he realized that, but that he felt that the time had come to be realistic and that in his judgment the main factor in [this] point was complete realism. Mr. Churchill then remarked that of course he was whole heartedly in favor of it and shared the President's view.

In connection with Roosevelt's views on an international organization, Welles later wrote:

The way the mind of the President was running at that time is shown in some notes which I made on August 11, during the time of the Atlantic Charter meeting, of a conversation which I had with the President on the afternoon of that day:

I said I had been surprised and somewhat discouraged by a remark that the President had casually made in our morning's conference, which was that nothing could be more futile than the reconstitution of a body such as the Assembly of the League of Nations. I said to the President that, if he conceived of the need for a transition period upon the termination of the war, during which period Great Britain and the United States would undertake the policing of the world, it seemed to me that it would be enormously desirable for the smaller powers to have available to them an Assembly in which they would all be represented, in which they could make their complaints known, and in which they could join in recommendations as to the policy to be pursued by the major powers who were doing the police work. I said it seemed to me that an organization of that kind would be the most effective safety valve that could be devised.

The President said that he agreed fully with what I said and that all that he had intended by the remark which he had made in the morning was to make clear his belief that a transition period was necessary, and that during that transition period no organization such as the Council or the Assembly of the League could undertake the powers and prerogatives with which they had been entrusted during the existence of the

League of Nations.

I further said that, while from the practical standpoint I was in agreement that the United States and Great Britain were the only powers which could or would exercise the police work, it seemed to me that it would be impossible to exclude from the responsibilities involved the other American Republics or, for that matter, such occupied countries as Norway, the Netherlands, and even Belgium.

The President replied that he felt that a solution for this difficulty could probably be found through the ostensible joining of those powers to Great Britain and the United States but that it would have to be recognized that this must be only ostensible, since none of the nations mentioned would have the practical means of taking any effective or at least considerable part in the task involved.

Perhaps because Welles believed that an international organization was very important he tried to justify his chief's apparent opposition to it by writing:

Franklin Roosevelt had by no means that "one track mind," which Woodrow Wilson once insisted he himself possessed. But he was always inclined to segregate the urgent from the not-so-urgent. He always preferred to devote himself to the task which was immediate rather than to the task which could be undertaken later on. It was, I think, only in that sense that during the Atlantic meeting he refused to consider urgent the need to reach a decision as to the precise kind of international organization to be created after the defeat of the Axis powers. . . . In August, 1941, his attention was fixed upon the defense of the United States. But clearly he was already convinced that the new American foreign policy, set forth in the Atlantic Charter, would later on be of great help in laying the foundations for a free and a secure world, and that the Atlantic Charter in itself would, in the meantime, hold out to the enslaved peoples of the earth the assurance that such a world would be achieved.

Actually, the President's seeming lack of interest, at this time, in what would become the United Nations Organization probably had a twofold explanation. First, he recognized that isolationist sentiment in the United States was still widespread. While the Atlantic meeting was in progress Congress had approved the extension of the Selective Service Act by a majority of only a single vote. Any reference to an "international organization" would cause an uprising of protest among the people and in Congress. Also, this was machinery—and Roosevelt was interested in goals, not the machinery for reaching them.

However, wily Winston Churchill was a difficult man to beat down. He cabled the War Cabinet in London that the final point was

. . . most remarkable for its realism. The President undoubtedly contemplates the disarmament of the guilty nations, coupled with the maintenance of strong united British and American armaments both by sea and air for a long indefinite period.

Having regard to our views about the League of Nations or other international organization, I would suggest the following amendment after the word "essential": "pending the establishment of a wider and more permanent system of general security."

He will not like this very much, but he attaches so much importance to the Joint Declaration, which he believes will affect the whole movement of United States opinion, that I think he will agree.

By this time the draft was up to eight points. Churchill had suggested one on social justice, which Roosevelt readily accepted. Roosevelt suggested one of freedom of the seas which Churchill was happy to endorse. In its final form the Atlantic Charter read:

JOINT DECLARATION BY THE PRESIDENT AND
THE PRIME MINISTER

August 12, 1941

The President of the United States of America and the Prime Minister, Mr. Churchill, representing His Majesty's Government in the United Kingdom, being met together, deem it right to make known certain common principles in the national policies of their respective countries on which they base their hopes for a better future for the world.

First, their countries seek no aggrandizement, territorial or other.

Second, they desire to see no territorial changes that do not accord with the freely expressed wishes of the peoples concerned.

Third, they respect the right of all peoples to choose the form of government under which they will live; and they wish to see sovereign rights and self-government restored to those who have been forcibly deprived of them.

Fourth, they will endeavour, with due respect for their existing obligations, to further the enjoyment by all States, great or small, victor or vanquished, of access, on equal terms, to the trade and to the raw materials of the world which are needed for their economic prosperity.

Fifth, they desire to bring about the fullest collaboration between all nations in the economic field, with the object of securing for all improved labour standards, economic advancement, and social security.

Sixth, after the final destruction of the Nazi tyranny they hope to see established a peace which will afford to all nations the means of dwelling in safety within their own boundaries, and which will afford assurance that all the men in all the lands may live out their lives in freedom from fear and want.

Seventh, such a peace should enable all men to traverse the high seas and oceans without hindrance.

Eighth, they believe that all the nations of the world, for realistic as well as spiritual reasons, must come to the abandonment of the use of force. Since no future peace can be maintained if land, sea, or air armaments continue to be employed by nations which threaten, or may threaten, aggression outside of their frontiers, they believe, pending the establishment of a wider and permanent system of general security, that the disarmament of such nations is essential. They will likewise aid and encourage all other practicable measures which will lighten for peace-loving peoples the crushing burden of armaments.

There is not now—and there was not then—a very clear understanding of what the Atlantic Charter was. In a sense, it meant all things to all people. It is clear that it was not a treaty, nor a covenant; it was not a legal document of any kind. It bore no seals or ribbons and was never formally approved by the legislatures of either government. Although there is reference to it being signed on August 11, 1941, there is no description of a signing ceremony. It was typed and then mimeographed for simultaneous release to the press in both countries immediately on conclusion of the meeting.

Roosevelt obviously considered it more meaningful than Churchill. One of the President's speech writers, dramatist Robert Sherwood, later wrote in a biography of Harry Hopkins that officers of the British government "never regarded it as a formal State Paper; it was, to them, not much more than a publicity handout." It meant something more than this to Churchill, who in a cable to London urging its release said: "It would be most imprudent on our part to raise unnecessary difficulties. We must regard this as an interim and partial statement of war aims designed to assure all countries of our righteous purpose and not the complete structure which we should build after victory." Later he wrote:

The profound and far-reaching importance of this Joint Declaration was apparent. The fact alone of the United States, still technically neutral, joining with a belligerent Power in making such a declaration was astonishing. The inclusion in it of a reference to "the final destruction of the Nazi tyranny" (this was based on a phrase appearing in my original draft) amounted to a challenge which in ordinary times would have implied warlike action. Finally, not the least striking feature was the realism of the last paragraph, where there was a plain and bold intimation that after the war the United States would join with us in policing the world until the establishment of a better order.

However, a month after the Atlantic Charter was released, the Prime Minister assured Parliament that point three, on self-determination, did not apply to India or Burma or other relationships within the British Empire but only to European nations occupied by the Nazis.

Sumner Welles summarized his description of the drafting of the Atlantic Charter by writing:

The Atlantic Charter represented the first major reversal of the isolationist policy which the American people had been pursuing since the close of the First World War. It represented the first effort at joint leadership on the part of the two leading English-speaking democracies. It was the first assurance for a quarter of a century to the free peoples outside the New World that the United States had undertaken a positive, rather than a negative, foreign policy. Far more than that, it represented, as soon as the United States had been drawn into the war, the one policy of enlightened international cooperation upon which the peoples struggling against Axis domination could base their hopes for a better world of the future.

Actually the Charter was more than this. Although it was a statement of broad objectives rather than precise commitments, it went beyond the scope of the Covenant of

the League of Nations. The League was primarily concerned with the political and legal aspects of international
relationships. The Atlantic Charter emphasized that economic and social relationships must also be of universal
concern. And it provided a focus for concrete planning
within the government on the part that the United States
might play in the postwar world.

Reaction toward the Charter in the United States was
mixed, but generally favorable. Many considered it a holy
document. *The Atlanta Constitution* ranked it with the
Magna Carta and the United States Constitution. *The
New York Times* saw "the beginning of a new era." On
the other hand, many papers considered it as merely a pre-
lude for taking the country into war. The *Louisville
Courier-Journal* headlined, "America Stands Committed." Surprisingly, the *Christian Century* took a dim view
of the pious reverence with which the Atlantic meeting
was treated and sarcastically quipped, "one thinks immediately of a certain meeting which is supposed to have
taken place on Mount Sinai."

One rather surprising reaction to the Charter, from
those who endorsed it, was the criticism that it mentioned
only two of the Four Freedoms—want and fear. F.D.R.
thought it necessary to cover this omission when he presented the document to Congress by saying. "It is also unnecessary for me to point out that the declaration of principles includes of necessity the world need for freedom of
religion and freedom of information. No society of the
world organized under the announced principles could
survive without these freedoms, which are a part of the
whole freedom for which we strive."

Shortly after it was released, Roosevelt sought the support of Pope Pius XII for the Atlantic Charter. His memorandum to his personal representative at the Vatican, Myron C. Taylor, discloses some of his thinking at that time on the postwar world. The first two points which he stressed were those which he always considered most important—disarmament and equal economic opportunity. He put disarmament first, "because German, Italian and Japanese official policy and also psychology place control of other nations and peoples on the basis of armed force." But disarmament "by uniform voluntary methods" might take "generations" to accomplish, so "for some time" the nonaggressive nations "must be in a position to enforce nonaggression."

He instructed Taylor to talk to the Pope about freedom of religion, specifically in terms of Russia, whose attack on the church, he said, was aimed chiefly at removing it from politics. He added that he was also "definitely bearing in mind the possibility of persuading the Government of Russia ultimately to accept freedom of religion."

Two other points that he made reflect his views on world organization under the new order. One had to do with self-determination and plebiscites. He told Taylor:

The self-determination of boundaries and forms of governments was the most substantial contribution made by the Versailles Treaty—i.e., the plebescite method, which, on the whole, was successful. This method can be extended in the case of certain populations and areas which have conducted century-old feuds. . . . If there was . . . a plebiscite resulting in a close vote, with resulting recriminations, arrangements could be made for a later plebiscite or later plebiscites—the thought being that the method is not of necessity a final one. The whole point of this is that peaceful determination is a continuing process and thereby eliminates determination by war.

The other point was his favorite theme of trusteeship, on which he wrote:

In the present complete world confusion, it is not thought advisable at this time to reconstitute a League of Nations which, because of its size, makes for disagreement and inaction. There should be a meeting place of nations for the purpose of full discussion, but for management there seems no reason why the principle of trusteeship in private affairs should not be extended to the international field. Trusteeship is based on the principle of unselfish service. For a time at least there are many minor children among the peoples of the world who need trustees in their relations with other nations and peoples, just as there are many adult nations or peoples which must be led back into a spirit of good conduct.

Although Roosevelt did not specifically say so, he obviously believed that plebiscites, trusteeships, and disarmament should be supervised by the major powers. At the time of the Atlantic Charter this was thought of in terms of an Anglo-American police force. Later, Roosevelt talked in terms of a concept of "Four Policemen"—Russia and China were added.

Nothing was said about either Russia or China in this connection at the Atlantic meeting. In the case of China this is perhaps understandable in the face of the desire to avoid—or at least postpone—war with Japan. Russia was ignored, first, because it would have been impossible to get Soviet approval in time to issue the document as Roosevelt wanted to. More important, as a result of decisive German victories in Russia during the first weeks of their invasion, nobody, with the possible exception of Harry Hopkins, anticipated that the U.S.S.R. would last out the year.

Russia, together with the British Dominions and the

European governments in exile, formally went on record in support of the principles of the Atlantic Charter at a meeting in London in September, 1941. Many who were suspicious of Russia took heart at parts of the statement made by the Soviet ambassador at this time, in which he said that Soviet foreign policy was guided by "the principles of self-determination of nations . . . one of the pillars on which the political structure of the U.S.S.R. is built"; and that his government "defended the right of every nation to its independence, its territorial integrity, and to such a social order and form of government as it deems opportune and necessary."

No one seems to have paid much attention to the ambassador's qualification of this statement, to which italics have been added:

Considering that the practical application of these principles [of the Atlantic Charter] *will necessarily adapt itself to the circumstances, needs, and historic peculiarities of particular countries,* the Soviet Government can state that a consistent application of these principles will secure the most energetic support on the part of the Government and peoples of the Soviet Union.

In short, Russia endorsed the Atlantic Charter with its fingers crossed.

The Charter took another step forward in January, 1942, when immediately after the United States entered the war, Secretary of State Hull drafted a declaration of purpose for all the anti-Axis allies to sign. At this time there were more than two dozen; nine Latin American states had followed the United States into the war. There was some question as to what these nations should be called. "Alliance" was suggested, but it was thought that this would not sit well with the United States Congress, which traditionally thought of alliances in terms of "entangling"—something which George Washington had warned against. Churchill thought that "Associated Powers" was weak, and Roosevelt came up with the inspired title "Declaration of the United Nations." Thereafter, until neutrals were admitted, the United Nations simply comprised those states which were fighting the Axis powers. The first agency to bear the name was one that had been called the "Inter-Allied Information Center," which became the "United Nations Information Office."

The method of signing the declaration established a precedent that would be followed throughout the negotiations on the United Nations Organization. Although Roosevelt said that it would be "a distinct advantage to have as long a list of small countries as possible in this declaration," he agreed that the names of the four major powers should be placed at the head of the list, out of alphabetical order. "I have a feeling," he commented, "that the U.S.S.R. would not be pleased to see their names following some of the countries which are realistically making a minor contribution."

Some of the small states did not like this. Nor did they like the fact that the United States, Great Britain, China, and the U.S.S.R. signed at a ceremony at the White House on New Year's Day and the other twenty-seven signatory states signed at the State Department on the following day. This treatment of the smaller states as second-class citizens would be a stumbling block throughout the entire period of the formation of the United Nations Organization. But Roosevelt believed, quite realistically, that in the family of nations there were seniors and juniors—and the success of any international organization would depend on the seniors.

After some other minor disputes—including British objection to including India as a signatory and granting China the status of a major power—all of the countries which were fighting the Axis finally signed the:

DECLARATION BY UNITED NATIONS

A JOINT DECLARATION BY THE UNITED STATES OF AMERICA, THE UNITED KINGDOM OF GREAT BRITAIN AND NORTHERN IRELAND, THE UNION OF SOVIET SOCIALIST REPUBLICS, CHINA, AUSTRALIA, BELGIUM, CANADA, COSTA RICA, CUBA, CZECHOSLOVAKIA, DOMINICAN REPUBLIC, EL SALVADOR, GREECE, GUATEMALA, HAITI, HONDURAS, INDIA, LUXEMBOURG, NETHERLANDS, NEW ZEALAND, NICARAGUA, NORWAY, PANAMA, POLAND, SOUTH AFRICA, YUGOSLAVIA.

The Governments signatory hereto,

Having subscribed to a common program of purposes and principles embodied in the Joint Declaration of the President of the United States of America and the Prime Minister of the United Kingdom of Great Britain and Northern Ireland dated August 14, 1941, known as the Atlantic Charter.

Being convinced that complete victory over their enemies is essential to defend life, liberty, independence and religious freedom, and to preserve human rights and justice in their own lands as well as in other lands, and that they are now engaged in a common struggle against savage and brutal forces seeking to subjugate the world, DECLARE:

(1) Each Government pledges itself to employ its full resources, military or economic, against those members of the Tripartite Pact and its adherents with which such government is at war.

(2) Each Government pledges itself to cooperate with the Governments signatory hereto and not to make a separate armistice or peace with the enemies.

The foregoing declaration may be adhered to by other nations which are, or which may be, rendering material assistance and contributions in the struggle for victory over Hitlerism.

Done at Washington

January First, 1942.

On to Teheran

In the dark days of early 1942 peace seemed a long way off. The Germans had reached a point forty miles short of Moscow before they were stalled by snow, mud, and cold. The Japanese had conquered Burma, the Philippines, Indonesia, and Malaya; and Australia seemed to be in dire danger. Obviously, the first thoughts of the United Nations leaders were of fighting the war. Yet, even at this time the United States State Department was planning for a peaceful postwar world.

This planning was first undertaken by a committee initially headed by Sumner Welles—later by Secretary of State Cordell Hull—which included State Department officials, experts from outside government, and representatives from the Senate and House. Roosevelt well remembered that the refusal of the United States to join the League of Nations had been caused largely by Woodrow Wilson's

failure to include the Congress in his planning and negotiations. The World War I President had sailed off for
France without any representatives of the legislative body
and come back with the Covenant as a *fait accompli*. The
Senate felt that it should have been consulted; the Constitution provides that the upper house must advise and consent on such things. As a result, since they had not been
asked to advise, they did not consent.

F.D.R. did not intend to make the same mistake. Members of both houses were involved in or kept informed on
postwar planning at every step of the way, so that when
recommendations were finally made by the executive
branch they frequently *followed* resolutions that had already been introduced in the legislature.

Early planning on some aspects of the postwar world
were complicated by dissension between various groups in
the executive branch of the government. The Treasury
Department obviously had some ideas on economics and
finance and did not always agree with the State Department. Also, an Executive Committee on Economics had
been appointed independent of either department which
felt that this aspect of postwar planning was in their jurisdiction and disagreed violently with State. And the Departments of Labor and Agriculture believed that they
should have something to say. In the early stages, this made
it somewhat difficult for the British and the foreign governments in exile in London to know with whom they
should deal.

F.D.R. cut through some of the red tape by announcing,
early in 1943, that an international conference would be
held that spring to consider long-term food problems. He
may have picked up this idea from the work of an unoffi-

cial group of Australians, Canadians, British, and Americans which supported a "United Nations Program for Freedom from Want of Food." Mrs. Roosevelt had become interested in this and had arranged for the group's chairman to meet the President. The food conference, in Hot Springs, Arkansas, was actually the first formal United Nations meeting on a nonmilitary subject and resulted in the later establishment of the United Nations Food and Agriculture Organization. It was also the first time at which other than belligerent states were included in the United Nations. Thirteen neutral nations were invited to attend. These, with five later signers of the Declaration of the United Nations, brought membership up to forty-four states.

Roosevelt insisted that the agenda of the conference be limited to consideration of problems of long-term nutrition. This presented some difficulties—everybody else wanted to talk about food in terms of postwar relief. The President was adamant. Obviously, the bulk of postwar relief would have to be paid for by the United States, and F.D.R. did not want the first international meeting on the postwar world to deal with a subject which would provide such fine fuel for the isolationists. The food conference would—and did—produce recommendations in terms of broad generalizations and long-term planning which were far more palatable to public opinion.

Meanwhile the State and Treasury Departments had been working with the British and the governments in exile on plans for relief and rehabilitation and had completed a draft recommendation which was approved by Russia and China. After the food conference this was submitted to the other United Nations and made public. As the President anticipated, it met some opposition. Republican Senator Arthur Vandenberg saw it as "a preview of the method by which the President and the State Department intend [to settle] every possible war and post-war issue," and added that it "pledged our total resources to whatever illimitable schemes for relief and rehabilitation all around the world our New Deal crystal gazers might desire to pursue." A modification of the first draft which spelled out that Congress would control appropriations for relief and rehabilitation mollified Congress, and in November, 1943, the President signed a draft which brought UNRRA into being—the United Nations Relief and Rehabilitation Administration.

This was another step forward. The United States could well have taken the position that it would administer its great contributions to relief unilaterally. Instead, it chose to place them under the control of a United Nations agency in which other nations would have a voice. In signing, F.D.R. made it clear that his country would remain a full-fledged participant in postwar international affairs by saying: "We have worked together with the United Nations in full agreement and action in fighting on land, on sea, and in the air. We are now about to take an additional step in the combined actions which are necessary to win the war and to build the foundation for a secure peace."

These activities in specialized areas indicated Roosevelt's thinking, in early 1943, on postwar international organizations. On January 1, the anniversary of the signing of the Declaration of the United Nations, he said at a press conference, "the most important war objective . . . is to maintain peace . . . Almost all the other things we hope to get out of the war are . . . dependent on the maintenance of peace." When he was asked *how* he thought peace might be maintained he replied, "No, no . . . you are talking about details, I am talking about objectives . . . The details are not the important thing. This issue is: the objective."

He was still thinking in terms of the "Four Policemen" —the United States, Great Britain, Russia, and China—the only countries that, in his opinion, should maintain offensive armaments in the postwar world. The aggressors would be completely disarmed and all other states would have but token forces. He mentioned the possibility of a "watchdog" commission of small states that would inspect disarmament and report to the major powers any violations or signs of aggression.

He believed that there should be several autonomous agencies to deal with nonmilitary phases of international cooperation—such as food and agriculture, UNRRA, etc. He was rather vague as to how these should be bound together in an overall international organization—or whether they should be so combined. As he repeatedly said, this was not important—this was machinery.

In April of 1943 he sent up a trial balloon by permitting an article to be published in the *Saturday Evening Post* entitled "Roosevelt's World Blueprint," written by Forrest Davis with the tacit approval of the President. In this Davis made the statement that the President hoped "that the wartime alliance known as the United Nations may be developed into a society of free states, less ambitious and constraining than the League of Nations, but organic and capable of growth." But he added that he opposed "resurrecting the League or using Geneva as the capital of a world society, because of the aura of failure overhanging that city." Davis wrote:

> To Mr. Roosevelt, the subsidiary commission is the administrative crux of a United Nations world. A security commission made up of Russia, Britain and the United States might well police the peace of Europe during the transition period until the political reorganization of the Continent is completed. A similar commission including China could do the same for Asia. Subsidiary bodies could be entrusted with political reorganization. A sort of master commission, with each region represented, might sit permanently as an executive council on problems of friction between nations that might lead to war. The problem of raw material surpluses, of currency, tariffs, and so on, also could be delegated to commissions. These might have their headquarters anywhere in the United Nations—in Buffalo, Singapore, or Kiev.

When all the memoirs and commentaries of the time are studied it seems that F.D.R. discussed different ideas with different people, each of whom recorded his own view of the President's position. And others had more definite ideas including, within the administration, Cordell Hull and Sumner Welles. These statesmen both favored a single world organization of some kind. Welles favored a regional grouping of smaller states within the overall organization. On this Hull disagreed.

With the President's approval, the State Department set up a committee to study the problems of forming such an organization. This group came up with a tentative proposal for an interim United Nations Authority to function until the establishment of peace. This was to have an executive committee consisting of the four major powers and a few representatives from the other states, one from

each region. The regions were defined, somewhat vaguely,
as Eastern Europe, Western Europe, the American Republics, the Far East, and "possibly" the Mohammedan peoples. This was to be called the Provisional Armistice Administration and was to report from time to time in some
unspecified way to the full United Nations Authority so
that the nations not represented on the executive committee would have some idea of what was going on.

Although there were no formal international conversations on organization, British and American officials discussed the matter unofficially. Late in 1942 the British
Foreign Office sent to the War Cabinet a proposal which it
had been "elaborating in consultation with the State Department in Washington." This simply set forth, under
the title "The Four Power Plan," the suggestion that the
supreme direction of a postwar organization should be in
the hands of a council composed of the four major powers.
Churchill, like Roosevelt, believed that detailed planning
was premature—but he did have some ideas of his own. Of
the Four Power Plan he wrote Foreign Minister Anthony
Eden:

> It sounds very simple to pick out these four Big Powers. We
> cannot however tell what sort of a Russia and what kind of
> Russian demands we shall have to face. A little later on it may
> be possible. As to China, I cannot regard the Chungking Gov-
> ernment as representing a great world Power. Certainly there
> would be a faggot vote on the side of the United States in any
> attempt to liquidate the British Overseas empire.
>
> I must admit that my thoughts rest primarily in Europe.
> . . . It would be a measureless disaster if Russian barbarism
> overlaid the culture and independence of the ancient States of
> Europe. Hard as it is to say now, I trust that the European

family may act unitedly as one under a Council of Europe.
. . . It would be easy to dilate upon these themes. Unhappily
the war has prior claims on your attention and on mine.

Then the Prime Minister wrote, and sent to the President, a memorandum entitled "Morning Thoughts. A
Note on Postwar Security." The important paragraph of
this read:

It is the intention of the Chiefs of the United Nations to
create a world organization for the preservation of peace,
based upon conceptions of freedom and justice and the revival
of prosperity. As a part of this organization an instrument of
European government will be established which will embody
the spirit but not be subject to the weakness of the former
League of Nations. The units forming this body will not only
be the great nations of Europe and Asia Minor as long established, but a number of Confederations formed among the
smaller States, among which a Scandinavian Bloc, a Danubian
Bloc, and a Balkan Bloc appear to be obvious. A similar instrument will be formed in the Far East, with different membership, and the whole will be held together by the fact that
the victorious powers intend to continue fully armed, especially in the air, while imposing complete disarmament upon
the guilty. No one can predict with certainty that the victors
will never quarrel among themselves, or that the United States
may not once again retire from Europe, but after the experi-
ences which all have gone through, and their sufferings, and
the certainty that a third struggle will destroy all that is left of
the culture, wealth, and civilization of mankind and reduce us
to the level almost of wild beasts, the most intense effort will
be made by the leading powers to prolong their honourable
association and by sacrifice and self-restraint win for themselves a glorious name in human annals. Great Britain will
certainly do her utmost to organize a coalition resistance to
any act of aggression committed by any Power, and it is believed that the United States will cooperate with her, and even

possibly to take the lead of the world, on account of her numbers and strength, in the good work of preventing such tendencies to aggression before they break into open war.

Churchill elaborated on this regional organization because he said that the League of Nations had proved that "it was only the countries whose interests were directly affected by a dispute who could be expected to apply themselves with sufficient vigour to secure a settlement." In conversations in Washington he proposed that the world should be organized in three regional councils: one for the Western Hemisphere, one for Europe, and one for the Pacific. Representatives of these, together with the major powers, would form a Supreme World Council. He hoped that the United States would be represented in all three regional councils; Canada would represent the British Commonwealth in the Western Hemisphere, and Great Britain and the Soviet Union would be on the European and Pacific councils. He emphasized that "the last word would remain with the Supreme World Council, since any issues that the Regional Councils were unable to settle would automatically be of interest to the World Council. . . . The central idea of the structure was that of a three legged stool—the World Council resting on three Regional Councils."

The idea of the United States being a member of a regional body outside of the Western Hemisphere did not sit well at the White House or in the State Department. Although public opinion had progressed somewhat in terms of internationalism, the thought of the United States being a member of a European organization which was primarily political was still too radical to be considered.

Although the Americans and British were working together toward the same general overall purpose in planning a postwar world, there were many things on which they did not see eye to eye. Churchill was reluctant to agree that China should be considered as a major power. In his mind the Chinese were having very little influence in the war and were not capable of being one of the postwar policemen. Roosevelt thought differently. He considered close and friendly relations between China and the United States vital to American foreign policy in the East. Chiang Kai-shek's Nationalist government must be encouraged to remain in the war, the President believed, not only to contain Japanese forces that were fighting in China but to possibly provide bases for American attack.

Also, Roosevelt thought that the policemen should not all be Caucasians; it would be difficult to police Asia without the aid of an Asiatic country. And finally, the President asked the Prime Minister to visualize what might happen in Asia and the Pacific area if mammoth China ever got her hands on modern weapons and went the way of Japan. On this, current history may be proving his thinking prophetic. Regardless of the fact that the country was backward technologically, Roosevelt believed that China must be considered as a major power.

The two leaders also disagreed on the role that France should play in the postwar world. Churchill feared a Europe in which Russia would be the only major power. He said that "the prospect of no strong country on the map between England and Russia was not attractive." He wanted France rearmed to play her traditional role in the European balance of power.

At the time there were two French governments. The Vichy French government in unoccupied France was more or less at the mercy of its German conquerors. The United States had recognized this government in the hope of exerting some influence against its voluntary cooperation with Germany. The Free French government, led by Charles de Gaulle, was not popular in Washington. De Gaulle was as difficult to get along with in the 1940's as in the 1960's. Churchill recorded:

A very stern mood developed in Washington about De Gaulle. Not a day passed that the President did not mention the subject to me. Although this was done in a most friendly and often jocular manner, I saw he felt very strongly indeed upon it. Almost every day he handed me one or more accusing documents against De Gaulle from the State Department or the American Secret Service.

The Free French had embarrassed the United States by wresting control of St. Pierre and Miquelon, islands in the Western Hemisphere, from the Vichy government. This conflicted with the announced Pan-American policy of not permitting any change in the status of the Western Hemisphere possessions of European powers. But to correct the situation would have meant taking military action against the Free French, who were fighting the Axis. Such action would have been most unpopular with the British and the governments in exile. More important, Roosevelt saw no reason why France should have a strong military force after Germany was disarmed. He tended to lump France with the small European states which would be disarmed after the war.

The most important difference of opinion between the United States and Great Britain had to do with colonialism. The British government—and particularly Churchill himself—violently opposed any radical postwar change in British colonies. Churchill had growled that "he did not intend to preside over the liquidation of the British Empire." In the eyes of the United States his attitude was a direct refutation of point three of the Atlantic Charter.

When the United States Office of War Information suggested a joint statement on the anniversary of the Atlantic Charter and drafted a tentative announcement, the Prime Minister hurriedly cabled the President, saying:

I hope you will let me see beforehand the text of any message you are thinking of sending me upon the anniversary of the Atlantic Charter. We considered the wording of that famous document line by line together and I should not be able, without mature consideration, to give it a wider interpretation than was agreed between us at the time. Its proposed application to Asia and Africa requires much thought. Grave embarrassment would be caused to the defence of India at the present time by such a statement as the Office of War Information has been forecasting. In the Middle East the Arabs might claim by majority they could expel the Jews from Palestine, or at any rate forbid all further immigration. . . . This is only one of the many unforeseen cases which will arise form new and further declarations. . . . I am sure you will consider my difficulties with the kindness you always show me.

Roosevelt was convinced that the end of the war would bring a great upsurge in nationalism on the part of colonial peoples—although it is doubtful that even he envisioned that this would be as strong as it actually was. In 1942 the President told Soviet Foreign Minister Maxim Molotov, "the white nations . . . could not hope to hold these areas as colonies in the long run." The Netherlands East Indies, he said, "would some day be ready for self-government, and the Dutch know it." He talked more about Asian colonies than African, and he thought that each of the Southeast Asian territories would require "a different lapse of time before achieving readiness for self-government, but a palpable surge toward independence was there just the same."

Everybody in the United States government was against colonialism in principle; but there was great difference of opinion as to what should be done about it. Only Vice President Henry Wallace favored immediate postwar independence for all subject peoples, and his opinions on foreign affairs were not highly regarded. Secretary of State Cordell Hull's opinion was at the other extreme, and at the time he favored nothing more than a commitment on the part of imperial governments to the principle of ultimate independence for their colonies, after a period of preparation. Roosevelt was in the middle with his favorite international trusteeship idea.

The dissension within the government was made public when Under Secretary of State Sumner Welles made a speech in which he said:

If this war is in fact a war for the liberation of peoples, it must assure the sovereign equality of peoples throughout the world as well as in the world of the Americas. Our victory must bring in its train the liberation of all peoples. Discrimination between peoples because of their race, creed, or color must be abolished. The age of imperialism is ended. The right of a people to their freedom must be recognized as the civilized world long since recognized the right of an individual to his personal freedom. The principles of the Atlantic Charter must be guaranteed to the world as a whole—in all oceans and in all continents.

Welles was promptly pulled up short by his chief, Cordell Hull, with a statement which said, "We have always believed that all peoples, without distinction of race, color, or religion, who are prepared and willing to accept the responsibilities of liberty, are entitled to its enjoyment." He pointed out that the United States had "striven to meet squarely our own responsibility in this respect," and added that it would always be the policy of this country "to use the full measure of our influence to support the attainment of freedom by all peoples who, by their acts, show themselves worthy of it and ready for it." The only area for which any responsible person in government proposed immediate, or early, postwar independence was India. It was believed that territories like Indonesia, Indochina, and Korea would require a period of preparation. Nothing was said about the more backward colonial peoples in Africa.

In 1943 the State Department drafted a "Declaration by the United Nations on National Independence," which represented the United States policy at the time. This statement proposed United Nations trusteeship for League of Nations mandates and other territories which might be detached from the Axis powers. For other colonies it merely proposed a five-step procedure which should be adopted by all imperial governments. These steps included assurance that such governments would give colonial peoples protection, encouragement, moral support, and material aid to advance educationally, politically, economically, and socially; that they would make positions in government available to qualified colonials; that they would progressively grant such measures of self-government as the colonial people were ready for; that, as soon as possible, they would fix specific dates for independence; and that they would pursue economic policies favorable to the marketing of colonial resources.

When Roosevelt approved this it was hoped that it would be endorsed by all of the other United Nations; but it bogged down with the British. After lengthy discussions with Anthony Eden, Cordell Hull reported:

> The Foreign Secretary said that, to be perfectly frank, he had to say that he did not like our draft very much. He said it was the word "independence" that troubled him, he had to think of the British Empire system, which was built on the basis of Dominion and colonial status. He pointed out that under the British Empire system there were varying degrees of self-government, running from the Dominions through the colonial establishments which had in some cases, like Malta, complete self-government, to backward areas that were never likely to have their own government.

Unfortunately, after the failure of these efforts, no really effective United Nations policy on colonies was ever developed.

One minor aspect of a postwar United Nations organization on which F.D.R. had very definite ideas was the location of its headquarters. He wanted no such elaborate complex as the League of Nations had maintained in Geneva. He believed that the various subagencies might meet in different places around the globe; not necessarily always in the same place. If there was a general assembly he thought that it should not be headquartered in a large city where it would be subject to pressure from press and local public opinion; and it should not meet on the territory of one of the major powers. His choice for a headquarters was the Azores. This would be neutral territory for everybody. The islands were as mutually convenient as any other place yet sufficiently small and remote to make it possible to exclude unwarranted interference from the press and pressure groups which might interfere with or seek to sway the assembly's deliberations. Perhaps the last place in the world which met the President's qualifications for a United Nations headquarters was New York City.

Although Roosevelt, in 1943, was not primarily concerned with the definite machinery to guide the postwar world, others were. They remembered what had happened at the end of World War I when the American public—and its Congress—immediately lost interest in "making the world safe for Democracy" and were solely concerned with getting back to "normalcy"—a coined word which meant prosperity at home and let the rest of the world go hang. Reporting on a luncheon at the British Embassy, Churchill quoted U.S. Secretary of War Stimson as saying "most emphatically that in his opinion there would be a tendency to relax after hostilities ceased, and a reluctance to embark upon new international experiments. He believed that it would be much easier to secure American agreement during the war; indeed, that it was a case of during the war or never. The others were disposed to agree."

With the necessity in mind for securing, during the war, definite commitments for postwar organization, the State Department drafted a memorandum for the President in August, 1943. This posed several questions for decision, the most pertinent of which were:

1. Should we insist on the continuation of the present procedure of creating as we go along, *ad hoc* machinery for each particular short-run function and of leaving for the future the question of whether or not the separate pieces of machinery should be coordinated? Or should we press now toward the creation of some over-all United Nations agency to deal, through

appropriate component pieces of machinery, with all or most of the various functions involved?

2. Whichever course we select, should we agree that there should be a separate agency or set of agencies, for Europe and presumably another for the Far East? Or should we insist that European operations and Far Eastern operations be component parts of one general United Nations arrangement?

The President was not yet willing to move as fast as the Secretary of State proposed. He did approve of the drawing up of a "Tentative Draft of a Joint Four-Power Declaration, " which said, in part, that the major powers agreed: "That they recognize the necessity of establishing at the earliest practicable date a general international organization, based on the principle of the sovereign equality of all nations, and open to membership by all nations large and small, for the maintenance of international peace and security."

This was Roosevelt's first commitment to a "general international organization," to which he had refused to agree two years earlier in the Atlantic Charter. In this same document the United States took a firm position against the British proposal of regional organizations. The draft stated:

. . . (1) that the basis of international organization should be world-wide rather than regional; (2) that there are grave dangers involved in having the world organization rest upon the foundations of previously created, full-fledged regional organizations; and (3) that while there may be advantages in setting up regional arrangements for some purposes, such arrangements should be subsidiary to the world organization and should flow from it.

The draft concluded by stressing:

. . . the desirability of creating a general United Nations agency, operating on a functional basis and—when advisable—having some subsidiary regional structures. Such an agency could well be set up on a provisional basis during the war to perform concrete tasks involved in the transition from war to peace and to prepare the way for the establishment of a permanent world organization.

At the same time that this Four Power Declaration was prepared the House of Representatives went on record endorsing United States participation in a postwar international organization by passing the Fulbright Resolution which stated: "That the Congress hereby expresses itself as favoring the creation of appropriate international machinery, with power adequate to establish and to maintain a joint and lasting peace, among nations of the world, and as favoring participation by the United States therein through its constitutional processes." This was a historic milestone; the first time the Congress had ever approved of the participation of the United States in a political organization outside of the Western Hemisphere.

The main purpose of the Four Power Declaration was to feel out Russian opinion. The State Department memorandum which preceded the Tentative Declaration had made the point:

The sooner and the more fully we test out Moscow's intentions, the clearer will be our own tasks, as well as the possibilities open to us. Affording Moscow an opportunity to participate fully at all stages of preparation and action will provide an excellent test of this sort. . . . On the other hand, if it should happen that Moscow [is] reluctant to participate in a comprehensive procedure, the need for creating a closely knit agency of cooperation among the other United Nations will become even more emphatic.

The war had been going on for four years. Russia had been involved for over two years and the United States for more than a year and a half. But neither the United States nor Great Britain had yet been able to get a statement—no less a commitment—out of Russia on postwar aims. The British had been trying for two years to reach an Anglo-Soviet agreement, but Russia had held back unless the British agreed to recognize its territorial boundaries as of 1941; which meant an endorsement of the Russian grab of the Baltic States, part of Finland, and much of Poland. To this Churchill would not agree, and the United States threatened to disassociate itself publicly from any treaty which made such territorial commitments.

There had been numerous second-level conferences with the Russians. Harry Hopkins had visited Moscow for the United States and Anthony Eden for Great Britain. Maxim Molotov had visited Washington. In these meetings the conversations, particularly on the side of the Russians, had been primarily military. Roosevelt had been trying since 1942, without success, to set up a personal meeting with Joseph Stalin.

During 1943 the importance of getting some kind of a commitment from Russia was increasingly recognized. Hull said that it was "all-important to bring Russia in on a common determination to set up an international organization after the war. If an agreement were reached on this point, the settlement of other problems would be easier. If Russia refused, all other problems would be magnified."

In reply to several requests for a meeting from both Roosevelt and Churchill—and a joint request in August—Stalin insisted that he could not leave the war front, "even for one week." Instead he proposed, "it would be expedient to organize a meeting of the responsible representatives of our states." He insisted, "It is necessary beforehand to agree on the scope of the questions to be discussed and the drafts of the proposals which have to be accepted. The meeting will hardly give any tangible result without that."

When the Russians presented their proposed agenda for this meeting of Foreign Ministers—which they insisted take place in Moscow—it contained only one point, "the consideration of measures to shorten the duration of the war against Germany and her allies in Europe." To them this meant an Anglo-American guarantee of establishing a second front by an invasion of Europe. When Cordell Hull and Anthony Eden journeyed to Moscow in October, 1943, they took high-ranking military men, and Molotov would talk of nothing else until he had been assured that an invasion would be mounted in the spring of 1945.

After this assurance the Russians agreed that the Four Power Declaration proposed by the United States could be the second item on the agenda. Anthony Eden warmly supported the United States draft, although both he and Molotov protested at the inclusion of China, which was not represented at the meeting. Hull assured them that China had already approved. Molotov called for surprisingly few, and minor, changes, in what became the Moscow Declaration, which was signed by the three Foreign Ministers and the Chinese ambassador to Russia.

Hull reported that the Moscow Conference was an unqualified success because it "laid the foundation for cooperative effort in the post-war world toward enabling all peace-loving nations, large and small, to live in peace and security." Eden was not quite so enthusiastic, but he did say that the agreement to establish special machinery "over

and above the ordinary machinery of diplomatic inter-
change [represented] a great—perhaps the greatest—
achievement of the Conference." Stalin did not mention
this aspect of the meeting. He merely said that it was "elo-
quent evidence" that "our united countries are filled with
determination to deal the enemy common blows which
will result in final victory over him."

The Moscow Conference paved the way for the first
meeting of Roosevelt, Churchill, and Stalin in November
of 1943. The Russian dictator insisted that this be held in
Teheran, Iran, on the grounds that his responsibilities as
Commander-in-Chief of the Russian armies would not permit him to go farther from home. Roosevelt protested this
site because its remoteness took him out of touch with
events at home. But Stalin merely said that if the meeting
was not held in Teheran there would be no meeting,
thereby establishing an attitude that would continue
throughout the Anglo-American negotiations with the
U.S.S.R.

4

Good Old Uncle Joe

Roosevelt's bitter critics blame most of the bad things that have happened in the postwar world on his soft attitude toward communism and the faith that he had in the honesty and integrity of Joseph Stalin. His idolators claim that F.D.R.'s negotiations with the Russian dictator made possible the continuation of the United Nations after the war and that but for his diplomatic shrewdness the world would be in a much worse state. Sumner Welles, one of the latter, wrote:

Unquestionably Roosevelt's personal conferences with Stalin dispelled misconceptions and misunderstandings on both sides, and helped materially to pave the way for the successful elaboration of what later became the United Nations Charter. I agree with Robert Sherwood's estimate that, "If there was any supreme peak in Roosevelt's career, I believe it might well be fixed at this moment, at the end of the Teheran conference."

It is possible to trace some of the problems and mishaps of the postwar world to decisions made at Teheran and, later, at Yalta. Yet no one can say with certainty "what might have been" had these decisions been different.

First, it should be explained that, at the time, "Stalin," "communism," and "Russia" were synonymous. The Communist party controlled the Union of Soviet Socialist Republics—and Stalin was the unchallenged dictator of the Communist party. But there was an essential difference between Stalin and the other dictators. The Fascist party in Italy had been born and died with Mussolini. The Nationalist Socialist party—the Nazis—had been born and would die with Hitler. But the Communist party had been there long before Stalin and would continue long after Stalin, with an ideology unchanged since it was first preached by Karl Marx and made effective by Lenin.

And surely Roosevelt had read Lenin's statement:

> We are living not merely in a state, but in a system of states; and it is inconceivable that the Soviet republic should continue to exist for a long period side by side with imperialist states. Ultimately one or the other must conquer. Meanwhile a number of terrible clashes between the Soviet republic and the bourgeois states are inevitable.

To Lenin, any major state which was not communistic was imperialistic.

Roosevelt's unqualified acceptance of the Communists as potential good neighbors will always remain a mystery. He well knew that the communism of Marx and Lenin could never live side by side with democracy. Communism was dedicated to the overthrow of free enterprise and the human freedoms on which democracy is based. But Roosevelt thought that communism would change—that it was changing. And he believed that the capitalistic aspect of United States democracy should change, and he was doing much to bring this about. Communism is basically social-istic, and F.D.R. approved of the spread of many of the milder forms of socialism. His wife is the authority for the statement that "the President believed that the post-war world was going to be considerably more socialistic and he indicated no regrets about it."

Perhaps a good expression of his reason for believing that democracy and communism could exist peaceably in the postwar world was quoted by Sumner Welles:

He once said to me that he believed that if the world could remain at peace the following phenomenon would probably take place. He regarded the American form of democracy as being at the opposite pole from the original form of Soviet Communism. In the years which had elapsed since the Soviet revolution of 1917, the Soviet system had advanced ma-terially toward a modified form of state socialism. In the same way, the American policy since that time had progressed toward the ideal of true political and social justice. He be-lieved that American democracy and Soviet Communism could never meet. But he told me that he did believe that if one took the figure 100 as representing the difference between American democracy and Soviet Communism in 1917, with the United States at 100 and the Soviet Union at 0, American democracy might eventually reach the figure of 60 and the Soviet system might reach the figure of 40. The gap between these two final figures it seemed to him would never lessen.

Others have said that Roosevelt considered Stalin's regime as a rather "uncouth, Asiatic, New Deal."

Roosevelt's administration had been the first to recog-nize the Communist government, in 1933, and the Presi-dent told the first United States ambassador to Russia,

William Bullitt, that this recognition was partly inspired by his disgust with affairs in Europe and Japan and a hope that he might get Russia's cooperation in keeping the peace in Europe and Asia. As a result of his sojourn in Russia, Bullitt became convinced that United States–Soviet cooperation was impossible, and sent F.D.R. a strong memo to this effect shortly before the Teheran Conference. The President said that, while the ex-Ambassador's facts and logic made sense, "I just have a hunch that Stalin is not that kind of man. Harry [Hopkins] says he's not and that he doesn't want anything but security for his country, and I think if I give him everything I possibly can and ask nothing from him in return, *noblesse oblige,* he won't try to annex anything and will work with me for a world of democracy and peace."

Another aspect of Roosevelt's attitude toward communism during the war years had to do with many of the people around him. Communism became increasingly popular during the early 1940's with a certain class of intellectuals from which many of the President's advisers and State Department appointees were drawn. Roosevelt's ideas were influenced by advisers who, like Harry Hopkins, believed firmly in the merits of the Russian political system. The President could not know that some of his advisers were actually Russian agents. At one conference in Quebec he endorsed a plan drawn by Assistant Secretary of the Treasury Harry Dexter White, whom the F.B.I. later denounced as a Communist agent. At Yalta, the President was pictured with Alger Hiss standing smiling behind him. Hiss later served a prison sentence stemming from his trial for perjury that grew out of suspicions that he was a Soviet informer.

Another reason for F.D.R.'s apparent blindness on the subject of the Communists was his incurable optimism. Because he wanted something to happen which he considered good, he could see many reasons why it should happen. He pointed out that the record of the Soviet government for keeping the peace was unblemished except for its attack on Finland in 1939. After joining the League of Nations in 1934 Russia seemed to be working actively for peace until it was expelled in 1939 as a result of the Finnish incident. Roosevelt told the Pope that although the Soviet Union was as much of a dictatorship as Germany, the Russians never used anything but propaganda to spread their views.

He was sure that the Russians would continue to be un-aggressive. He wrote Admiral Leahy: "We need not worry about any possibility of Russian domination." He told General Stillwell, when the latter queried the possibility of Russia wresting Manchuria from China: "Stalin doesn't want any more ground. He's got enough. He could even put another hundred million people into Siberia." He told Secretary of Labor Frances Perkins: "You know I really think the Russians will go along with me about having no spheres of influence."

He publicly said that the Russians were not trying to "gobble up all the rest of Europe and the world" and did not have "any crazy ideas of conquest." He added: "They have got a large enough 'hunk of bread' right in Russia to keep them busy for a great many years to come without taking on any more headaches." At the end of 1943 the President told Welles that he had "the positive conviction that the Soviet government would in its own interests recognize that its security could best be assured, and its legitimate objectives most readily attained, by cooperating fully with the United States in a universal international organization."

Roosevelt's pragmatism also played an important role in his conciliatory attitude toward Russia. He was firmly convinced that his Four Policemen concept of maintaining world peace would be possible only if Russia was one of the policemen. Since this, in his opinion, was a necessity, the President was willing to compromise with his long-term ideals in order to meet the problem of the moment. He felt that Stalin and the Soviets had good cause to be suspicious of the outside world, and that they would co-operate if these suspicions were allayed. He believed that this could be done with Russia as it had been done with Latin America—by holding out both hands in friendship and leaning over backwards to avoid doing anything which might enhance the Soviet suspicions.

Elliott quoted his father as saying:

Even our alliance with Britain holds dangers of making it seem to China and Russia that we support wholly the British line in international politics. . . . The United States will have to *lead*, lead . . . and use our good offices always to conciliate, help to solve the differences which will arise between the others—between Russia and England, in Europe between the British Empire and China and between China and Russia, in the Far East. We will be able to do that, because we're big, and we're strong, and we're self-sufficient. Britain is on the decline, China—still in the eighteenth century. Russia—suspicious of us, and making us suspicious of her. America is the only great power that can make peace in the world stick. It's a tremendous responsibility. And the only way we can start living up to it is by getting to talk with these men, face-to-face.

Churchill considered Russian participation in a postwar organization as highly desirable and wrote that he felt "bound to proclaim [his] confidence in Soviet good faith in the hope of procuring it." However, he did not agree with Roosevelt's basic premise that an international organization could not be established without Russia and was not adverse to planning for such an organization if the Russians could not be brought in on terms which would make it impossible for them to thwart the purpose of the organization. Although the Prime Minister proclaimed his confidence in Russian good faith, Great Britain was as suspicious of Russian purposes as the Russians were of those of Great Britain.

According to Elliott, his father believed that Churchill was motivated by a selfish concern for the British Empire. He told his son, "Trouble is, the P.M. is thinking too much of the post-war and where England will be. He's scared of letting the Russians get too strong."

As to Stalin himself, Roosevelt was convinced that he could convert the Russian dictator to become a disciple of sweetness and light. F.D.R. was supremely confident—to the point of extreme egotism—of his ability to handle people. Before Teheran he wrote Churchill: "I think I can personally handle Stalin better than either your Foreign Office or my State Department. Stalin hates the guts of all your top people. He thinks he likes me better, and I hope he will continue to do so." Soon after he arrived in Teheran the President was referring to the Russian dictator as "Uncle Joe," and bragged gleefully that he had made the inscrutable Tartar smile. In view of later events it is amazing that he accepted Stalin's statements at

face value—something that he did not do even with Churchill. Here, again, his optimism is evident; the wish may have
been father to the thought. F.D.R. ignored that part of
Lenin's prescription for spreading communism in which
he said, "We must resort to artifices, evasions and sub-
terfuges."

After Teheran the President described Stalin in a radio
broadcast by saying, "He is a man who combines a tremendous, relentless determination with a stalwart good humor.
I believe he is truly representative of the heart and soul of
Russia; and I believe that we are going to get along very
well with him and the Russian people—very well indeed."
He is certainly the only one who ever found any "good
humor" in the Russian dictator.

Despite all of the rationalization, it is difficult to com-
prehend why Roosevelt went to such great lengths to conciliate Stalin, even to the point of offending Churchill. At
Teheran he lived in the Russian Embassy compound with
Stalin while Churchill stayed in the British Embassy. He
refused a luncheon invitation with Churchill on the
grounds that this would displease the Russians, and then
had a private meeting with Stalin. At one dinner Stalin
proposed a toast to the effect that German militarism must
be subdued by shooting fifty thousand captured German
officers. When Churchill replied that "the British Parliament and public will never tolerate mass executions,"
Roosevelt proposed a compromise—only forth-nine thousand would be shot. This was probably said in fun, but
Churchill left the room in the middle of dinner.

The President undertook to "sell" the Soviets to the
American people. One sore point, in the United States,

was Russian intolerance of religion. One of the Four Freedoms was religious freedom. When the question of Russian
atheism was raised at a press conference F.D.R. answered:

The President: As I think I suggested a week or two ago, some
of you might find it useful to read Article 124 of the Constitution of Russia.

Question: What does that say, Mr. President?

The President: Well, I haven't learned it by heart sufficiently
to quote—I might be off a little bit, but anyway: freedom of
conscience—freedom of religion. Freedom equally to use
propaganda against religion, which is essentially what is the
rule in this country; only, we don't put it quite the same
way.

For instance, you might go out to-morrow—to the corner of
Pennsylvania Avenue, down below the Press Club—and stand
on a soap-box and preach Christianity, and nobody would
stop you. And then, if it got into your head, perhaps the next
day preach against religion of all kinds, and nobody would
stop you.

Although the Soviets had adopted a constitution in 1935
the President certainly knew that in practice, in terms of
human rights for the Russian people, it was merely a scrap
of paper. Article 124 did provide that "freedom to perform
religious rights and freedom of anti-religious propaganda
is recognized for all citizens." But F.D.R. was certainly not
so naïve as to believe that the former freedom was actually
in effect except on a token basis. He had told Myron Taylor
to tell the Pope that he was trying to persuade Russia to
ultimately accept freedom of religion. His press conference
statement was another instance of expediency overruling
idealism.

En route to Teheran the President stopped at Cairo to
meet with Churchill and Chiang Kai-shek. F.D.R. pro-

posed to the Prime Minister that Stalin be requested to send Molotov and a Russian military adviser to this meeting. Churchill was "alarmed" at the idea of a Soviet general, with "no authority or power to speak except as instructed," who would "simply bay for an earlier Second Front and block all other discussions." He later wrote that Roosevelt's suggestion reflected "a strong current of opinion in American Government circles, which seemed to wish to win Russian confidence even at the expense of coordinating the Anglo-American war effort."

The discussions at the Cairo Conference were purely military except for an agreement to return to China such territories as Manchuria, Formosa, the Pescadores, which Japan had conquered; an agreement which contained the phrase: "The aforesaid three great powers, mindful of the enslavement of the people of Korea, are determined that in due course Korea shall become free and independent." After the conference Roosevelt wrote what turned out to be a most ironic prophecy: "I really feel that it is a triumph to have got the four hundred and twenty-five million Chinese in on the Allied side. This will be very useful twenty-five or fifty years hence."

At Teheran, Roosevelt opened the first conference session by suggesting that the the general staffs conduct military conversations while he, Churchill, and Stalin discussed postwar affairs. Stalin would have none of this. As a result, the formal meetings of the conference were devoted largely to the conduct of the war. Other matters were dealt with at meals and in private conversations between Roosevelt and Stalin or Churchill and Stalin.

At least one of the military decisions had a bearing on the organization of the postwar United Nations, in that it

influenced Russia's position at the time of final negotiations. And it had great bearing on the situation in postwar
Europe. Churchill and Roosevelt had already agreed that
the invasion of Northern France, across the English
Channel—then called OVERLORD—would take place
about May 1, 1944. Churchill now proposed delaying this
by not more than two months so that some Anglo-American forces in the Mediterranean could be employed in an
invasion of the Balkans. He hoped that this would bring
Turkey into the war on the side of the United Nations. In
any event it would support the partisans who were then active in this area and would draw off Axis troops from what
would later become the main front.

Stalin would not agree to any postponement of OVER-
LORD, and Roosevelt supported him. The President proposed that forces in the Mediterranean which could not be
employed in the invasion of northern France might make
a diversionary landing in southern France, across the
Mediterranean, shortly before OVERLORD. To this
Stalin agreed. All of this talk was purely in military
terms, but both Stalin and Churchill were motivated by
political considerations.

Churchill foresaw that, if no Anglo-American forces
were involved in the Balkans, the war would end with the
Communists in control of Bulgaria, Roumania, Yugoslavia, Hungary, Czechoslovakia, and perhaps Austria. This
was an eventuality which he did not relish. Stalin, while
talking of OVERLORD, was determined that Eastern Europe should end up in the Soviet sphere of influence and
probably already anticipated that these countries would be
reduced to Communist puppets or satellites behind what
Churchill later dubbed "the Iron Curtain." American

General Mark Clark was one of many who considered Roosevelt's agreement with Stalin a grave error. He wrote:

A campaign that might have changed the whole history of relations between the Western world and the Soviet Union was permitted to fade away. . . . Not alone in my opinion, but in the opinion of a number of experts who were close to the problem [this] . . . was one of the outstanding mistakes of the war. . . . Stalin knew exactly what he wanted . . . and the thing he wanted most was to keep us out of the Balkans.

At Teheran Roosevelt backed off from insistence on self-determination as called for in the Atlantic Charter and, for all practical purposes, disavowed his favorite theory of plebiscites. Again, he bowed to expediency in his efforts to placate the Russians and convince them that they would not be dominated by Anglo-American policy.

The Russians had taken over three Baltic states—Latvia, Lithuania, and Estonia—in 1939. When Roosevelt raised the question of self-determination for these people Stalin replied categorically "that the Baltic States had by an expression of the will of the people voted to join the Soviet Union and that this question was not therefore one for discussion." Roosevelt mentioned that world opinion, and opinion in the United States, was not satisfied because there had been no outside supervision of the Baltic plebiscites. Stalin said that there would be full opportunity for the people involved to express their will under the Soviet Constitution, and he would not agree to any form of international supervision.

Of more concern was the situation in Poland. At the same time that the Germans had invaded Poland from the west—and started World War II—the Russians had invaded from the east and occupied almost half the country. Later the Polish government in exile claimed that the Russians had massacred fifteen thousand Polish officer prisoners in the Katyn forest and demanded an investigation by the International Red Cross. As a result of this, Russia broke relations with the Polish government. Churchill was anxious to re-establish relations between the Russians and the Poles and to get a statement from Stalin on Polish postwar boundaries. Stalin's attitude was that perhaps Poland could have some of eastern Germany, but Russia intended to keep what it had. There was not even any talk of a plebiscite for the Poles. Roosevelt refused to meet with the Polish Premier before Teheran or to concede to his request that the President intervene in behalf of Poland.

Another military decision that was reached at Teheran which would have far-reaching political consequences in the postwar world, and which would involve the United States in its first United Nations police action, was the agreement by Stalin to declare war on Japan as soon as Germany was conquered. Later, at Yalta, when Japan was virtually defeated, Roosevelt encouraged him to fulfill this promise. As a result, Russian armies raced into Manchuria and North Korea in time to accept the surrender of Japanese forces in these areas—they did no fighting. The thirty-eighth parallel which divides North and South Korea was a line originally established to determine which Japanese forces should surrender to the Americans and which to the Russians.

The end result of this was that the Russians turned Manchuria over to the Chinese Communists—together with much Japanese arms and munitions—and established a Communist government in North Korea without a supervised plebiscite. This brought about the United Nations "police action" in Korea in the early 1950's—which cost the United States far more, in terms of both casualties and money, than the combined total of all the foreign wars in which the country had previously been engaged with the exception of the two World Wars.

Consideration of a postwar world organization at Teheran was limited to an informal talk between Roosevelt and Stalin. The ideas which the President outlined to the Russian called for a world-wide assembly comprising all the United Nations, which would meet at various places to discuss world problems and make recommendations for their solution. In addition, there should be a smaller executive committee composed of the Big Four plus representatives of various groups of countries: the British Dominions, the American Republics, and the European, Middle Eastern, and Far Eastern regions. Principally, the President talked about the Four Policemen, the enforcement body which would have authority to deal with any threat to the peace.

Stalin objected to the inclusion of China as a major power because it was not, in fact, a strong military power. Also, he claimed that the European states would resent an Asiatic state on the enforcement body. Although he at first suggested a regional system similar to that proposed by the British, he later changed his mind and agreed that some form of world-wide organization would be preferable. He made the point that the Four Policemen idea would involve sending American troops overseas, but Roosevelt insisted that the contribution of the United States could be limited to air and naval support of the armies of Russia and Great Britain. Nothing was said about what would happen if one of the major powers should become an aggressor.

No definite statement on postwar organization was contained in the Teheran Declaration. It merely reaffirmed the pledge of the Moscow Declaration that the three powers would work together "in war and the peace that will follow." Roosevelt considered Stalin's agreement to this effect as a long step forward. In a broadcast to the American people he said:

[At Teheran] we did discuss international relationships from the point of view of big, broad objectives, rather than details. But on the basis of what we did discuss, I can say even today that I do not think any insoluble differences will arise among Russia, Great Britain, and the United States. . . .

As long as these . . . nations with great military power stick together in determination to keep the peace there will be no possibility of an aggressor nation arising to start another world war. But those four powers must be united with and cooperate with all the freedom-loving peoples of Europe, and Asia, and Africa, and the Americas. The rights of every nation, large or small, must be respected and guarded as jealously as are the rights of every individual within our own Republic.

Churchill wrote, of the Teheran meeting:

The political aspects were at once more remote and speculative. . . . It would not have been right at Teheran for the Western democracies to found their plans upon suspicions of the Russian attitude in the hour of triumph and when all her dangers were removed. . . . The hope of the future lay in the most speedy ending of the war and the establishment of a World Instrument to prevent another war, founded upon the combined strength of the three Great Powers whose leaders had joined hands in friendship around the table.

Stalin said or wrote nothing.

Stalin's acquiescence at Teheran seemed to confirm the Moscow Declaration, which had ended by saying:

It was recognized as desirable that representatives of the United States of America, the United Kingdom, and the Soviet Union should conduct, in a preliminary fashion, an exchange of views on questions connected with the establishment of an international organization for the maintenance of international peace and security, the intention being that this work should be carried out in Washington and also in London and Moscow.

After Teheran the U.S. State Department concentrated on developing more definite plans for the establishment of such an organization, to be discussed at an early date with Great Britain and Russia. Secretary of State Hull proposed that the other members of the United Nations should be asked to adhere to point four of the Four Nation Declaration, which related to the postwar organization. Great Britain objected on the grounds that the smaller nations might raise, "a number of questions . . . relative to the nature of the organization, which it would be awkward to dispose of," and urged that the three powers should first "attempt . . . to draw up a more detailed and comprehensive document." Hull withdrew his suggestion to consult with the smaller states, a decision which would cause difficulties in later negotiations. In all of this preliminary planning China was rather off to the side. It was assumed that it would agree with anything that the United States proposed.

The committees that had been established in 1941 had by June, 1943, developed a "Draft Constitution of an International Organization," which provided for the regional form of representation favored by Welles. Hull did not like this, and differences of opinion between the Secretary and the Under Secretary led the latter to resign in the fall of 1943. A new committee drew up, in June, 1943, a document entitled a "Charter of the United Nations." This was the first time that such a designation was used, although the document was a long way from the final charter.

While further plans were being drawn for a general organization, the State Department sought to draft more definite proposals for other subsidiary organizations. Hull wanted to establish a big power Steering Committee in the area of postwar economics. The British objected; they were still concerned with Imperial Preference. The matter was shelved at that time, but United States thinking later resulted in the Economic and Social Council of the United Nations.

Conferences on finance led to the later establishment of the International Bank for Reconstruction and Development. A conference on international civil aviation led to the International Civil Aviation Organization. In the area of education and cultural activities the Conference of Allied Educational Ministers considered a United States proposal for merely a reconstruction agency as too narrow, and this subject was deferred, although the preliminary talks ultimately led to UNESCO—the United Nations Educational, Scientific, and Cultural Organization.

Another subject on which it was impossible to secure agreement was the postwar status of dependent peoples. Nobody but the United States wanted to talk about this, and there was still disagreement on the subject between the President and the State Department. Roosevelt was still strong for his international trusteeship idea. Hull favored merely a commitment for ultimate independence on the part of imperial governments.

British Ambassador Lord Halifax was disturbed because Roosevelt had been quoted as saying flatly that Indochina (now Laos, Cambodia, and Viet Nam) should not be returned to France. When Hull queried the President on this, F.D.R. replied with a memo which said:

I saw Halifax last week and told him quite frankly that it was perfectly true that I had, for over a year, expressed the opinion that Indo-China should not go back to France, but that it should be administered by an international trusteeship. France has had the country—thirty million inhabitants—for nearly one hundred years, and the people are worse off than they were at the beginning.

As a matter of interest, I am wholeheartedly supported in this view by Generalissimo Chiang Kai-shek and by Marshal Stalin. I see no reason to play in with the British Foreign Office in this matter. The only reason they seem to oppose it is that they fear the effect it would have on their own possessions and those of the Dutch. They have never liked the idea of trusteeship because it is, in some cases, aimed at future independence. This is true in the case of Indo-China. Each case must, of course, stand on its own feet, but the case of Indo-China is perfectly clear. France has milked it for one hundred years. The people of Indo-China are entitled to something better than that.

During the first half of 1944, four things were going on simultaneously: (1) military planning to win the war; (2) concern for the shape of Europe, in terms of territorial boundaries, after the war; (3) planning for subordinate international agencies; (4) planning for a general international organization. Everyone agreed that number one should come first, but there was a difference of opinion on the precedence of the other points. The State Department wanted to put point four next. Disagreement to this was expressed by the Republican leader in the Senate, Alfred Vandenberg, who wanted to see a "just" peace established in Europe before agreement was reached on the organization which would strive to keep that peace. Vandenberg agreed in principle with the draft proposal which the State Department presented in the spring of 1944, but he said:

. . . no matter how acceptable this program for a new League might be, everything depends upon the kind of peace—whether it is a *just* peace—which this new international organization will implement. We are all disturbed by Russia's unilateral announcements from time to time as to what she intends to do, for example, with Poland and the other Baltic States; and by Churchill's constant reiteration of restoring the British Empire intact. The *peace* will create a new status quo in the world. The new "League" will defend the new status quo. It is my position that the United States cannot subscribe to this defense, no matter how hedged about, unless and until we know more about what the new status quo will be.

Secretary Hull's position was that the American proposals for an international organization would "greatly facilitate the working out of a good peace rather than a bad peace." He added: "Otherwise, when the fighting is over, there will be no program halfway perfected even tentatively; our leadership will be gone; and each country will already be preparing to hoe its own row in the future."

All of this was further complicated by the fact that 1944 was a national election year. As practical politicians the President and members of both houses of Congress had to consider the feelings of large ethnic groups of voters. Ev-

Franklin Delano Roosevelt

Winston Churchill

President Harry S. Truman of the United States addressing the
16th Plenary Session of the San Francisco Conference on June 25,
1945.

A view of the Permanent Headquarters of the United Nations in
New York. The buildings are the 29-story Secretariat (right), the
General Assembly (background), and the Library (foreground).

Mr. Alex Quaison-Sackey, President of the General Assembly, (center, at the presidential rostrum) with Secretary-General U Thant (left), and Mr. C. V. Narasimhan, Under-Secretary for General Assembly Affairs and Chef de Cabinet, December 1, 1964.

A general view of the Security Council during a debate.

The flags of some of the member states of the United Nations in front of the façade of the U.N. Secretariat building.

United Nations

A view of the Headquarters of the United Nations against New York's mid-Manhattan skyline. The sky-scraper houses the Secretariat's offices; council chambers and conference rooms are located in the low building at the river's edge, and the General Assembly in the domed building at right.

erybody wanted to stay on the fence in connection with the shape of postwar Europe so as not to alienate Polish-Americans, Slavic-Americans, Lithuanian-Americans, etc. At Teheran the President had reminded Stalin that there were "six or seven million Americans of Polish extraction and others of Lithuanian, Latvian, and Estonian origin, who had the same rights and same votes as anyone else."

Another problem which started to raise its head in the spring of 1944, and which would become increasingly acute, was the attitude of the small states. They felt, with much justice, that the big powers were running with the ball and that the small states would be but pawns in any world organization which the large nations devised. In June the governments in exile of Luxembourg, the Netherlands, Belgium, and Norway sent a memorandum to the Big Three affirming their desire to participate in a world organization but requesting at least an unofficial exchange of views as to the nature of such an organization before final decisions were reached. Several of the Latin American nations were even more outspoken in their expressions to the United States.

American public opinion also affected planning at this time. Isolationism was still a potent force, and there was some feeling that the government was planning to sacrifice national sovereignty in the creation of a world superstate. This was heightened by a small but very vocal group which advocated just such a proposal. When Hull asked Roosevelt to issue a public statement to allay the fears of the small states and the isolationists the President said:

The maintenance of peace and security must be the joint task of all peace-loving nations. We have, therefore, sought to develop plans for an international organization comprising all such nations. The purpose of the organization would be to maintain peace and security and to assist, through international cooperation, the creation of conditions of stability and well-being necessary for peaceful and friendly relations among nations. . . .

We are not thinking of a superstate with its own police forces and other paraphernalia of coercive power. We are seeking effective agreement and arrangements through which the nations would maintain, according to their capacities, adequate forces to meet the needs of preventing war and of making impossible deliberate preparation for war.

The President had obviously come a long way from his original view of a "Four Policemen" organization to enforce peace on an otherwise disarmed world and a group of loosely organized autonomous agencies to handle other aspects of international relations. He now approved of something similar to the League of Nations, with broader concern for the economic and social welfare of the world and, hopefully, without the weaknesses of the League.

The greatest weakness of the League was that all of the major powers had not been members—specifically, the United States. For this reason the United States government never seriously considered, in its planning, a postwar organization that did not include Russia. Russia was cooperating in the war effort, although the path was far from smooth. At Moscow and Teheran the Russians had agreed to cooperate in the postwar world. Even those who took the darkest pessimistic view of Russian intentions agreed that the experiment would have to be tried. Internationalism offered a better opportunity for getting along with the Communists than a retreat to isolationism. And, in addition to Roosevelt's optimistic view of the Russians, there was the practical point that they would be faced, at

the end of the war, with such a tremendous internal reconstruction problem that they would, it was believed—or
hoped—play ball with the West in order to obtain
assistance in rebuilding their country.

Another weakness of the League was that it did not have
any practical enforcement machinery to keep the peace.
League members agreed to renounce war as an instrument
of national policy and to submit disputes to arbitration or
to the World Court. But what happened when a member
state did not honor its commitments under the League
Covenant was somewhat vague and very complicated.
Obviously, planning for the new postwar organization
must recognize the need for international machinery to
employ force against an aggressor. At the time, "aggressor"
and "Axis" were considered synonymous, and much short-
term planning dealt with means to prevent a resurgence of
German or Japanese militarism. Future aggression by a
small state presented no real problem, so long as the four
major powers were in agreement. Nobody liked to think
about what would happen if one of the big states were the
aggressor.

It was also recognized that the new organization must go
much farther than the League in the area of international
economics. The basic impetus toward war in Germany,
Japan, and Italy had been economic. The postwar United
Nations must concern itself with international efforts to increase free trade and to improve living and social standards
throughout the world—in short, to assure freedom from
want. Before the war much of the international machinery in such areas as health, labor, and food had been outside the League. It had not gone far enough, nor had it
worked very well. This was an added argument for coordi-

nating all such agencies within the new general organization.

The military and strictly political aspects of maintaining peace had been considered in the "Draft Constitution" prepared in the spring of 1943 and in the "Charter of the United Nations" (known by its working title of "Staff Charter") which succeeded the Draft Constitution. During the first half of 1944 these papers were the basis for the development of more definite proposals drafted by an Informal Political Agenda Group. This first resulted in an "Outline Plan" of an international organization for the President, which Roosevelt approved in February, 1944. This was followed by "Tentative Proposals for a General International Organization" to be submitted to the other major powers.

Although this planning was done within the State Department, this Agenda Group was assisted by a Committee of Eight from the Senate and influenced by ideas submitted by many private organizations: principally the Commission to Study the Organization of Peace, the Council of Foreign Relations, the American Association for the United Nations, the Federal Council of Churches of Christ in America, Americans United for World Organization, and the Foreign Policy Association.

5

The Meeting
at Dumbarton Oaks

Although it was generally accepted that the new international organization would perform several functions, by far the most important was considered to be the maintenance of peace in the world. Perhaps 90 percent of the time of the Agenda Group was devoted to this. What kind of an organization would be best for this purpose? How would it function? What powers should it have? If there were to be an international police force, how should it be constituted? Should it be supplied exclusively by the Big Four?

There were two aspects to maintaining the peace—enforcement and peaceful settlement. Both of these would require machinery. Should it be the same machinery or separate machinery? With war raging throughout the globe and all the world in arms, far more attention was paid to the enforcement aspect than to the subject of peaceful settlement. This latter did not come under careful scrutiny until late in the discussions. During most of the planning stage it was considered that the big, all-important function of an international organization would be the *enforcement* of peace; this far overshadowed all else.

It is interesting to trace the thinking that led to the Security Council of the United Nations. At first, most planning was based on Roosevelt's concept of the Four Policemen. All power and authority to enforce peace would be placed in the hands of the four major powers. There would probably be an international assembly of some kind, but this would be primarily a forum or debating society in which the small states could air their views. It would have no executive functions. As the President had said, the participation of the small states would be "ostensible."

Early in 1943 the State Department planners started to whittle away at this concept. It was obvious that the small states would not willingly accept it nor voluntarily participate in an international organization in which they had no voice and no authority in connection with even their own security. By the time the Draft Constitution was prepared the plan for an international organization had developed into a General Conference, a Council, and an Executive Committee. The General Conference would later become the Assembly of the United Nations, but in the early stages the word "Assembly" was avoided because of its unpleasant connotation in relation to the League. The General Conference was still considered as primarily a forum.

The Council was to consist of the four major powers and "some" of the smaller states—at various times any number from three to eleven were proposed. All authority would presumably lay in this Council, not only for security but for economic and other aspects of international relations. Membership in the Council seemed to give the small states a voice, but actually their presence was little more than window dressing. The Executive Committee consisted of only the Big Four, and actual authority lay with this group. The Council could do little more than approve the decisions of the Executive Committee.

Then the planners started to transfer powers from the Committee to the Council. By the time the Draft Charter was prepared the Committee had been shorn of so much of its authority that it was dropped as a separate entity. This was the end of the Four Policemen, or at least of any public recognition of this concept. But authority on economic and social aspects of international relations, trusteeships, and other matters was still vested in the Council, which was now called an Executive Council.

In the next step the Agenda Group started to transfer authority on matters not related to security from the Executive Council to the Assembly. The Council became what its final name implied, a Security Council. By the time the Tentative Proposals were formulated, the Assembly was the responsible organ of the organization for all except the enforcement of the peace and the settlement of disputes which might lead to a breach of the peace, although there were still some things outside these areas in which the Council could override the Assembly. Amendments to the charter of the international organization had to be ratified by the Council, which also had the right to approve new members.

What armed forces should be available to the Council for use in enforcing the peace was a major problem for the planners. Should there be an international military force accountable solely to the Council—a permanent United Nations police force? Or should each member state maintain specific units which would be immediately available to the United Nations? Or should each member supply contingents from its regular forces, of a size to be determined in each instance, when called upon to do so by the Council? Or should geography and other factors be taken into consideration in each instance of a breach of the peace and only certain members, depending mainly on their location, be asked to contribute armed forces on particular occasions?

The international police force concept received lengthy consideration, particularly in terms of a United Nations air force. Roosevelt had frequently maintained that peace could be enforced solely by air power. If a state did not behave, the policemen would threaten to bomb its principal cities. If it did not then fall in line, the threat might be carried out. There was much objection to this in principle as the war disclosed the indiscriminate nature of air bombardment. Bombers might be justified as weapons of war, but many felt that they would not be justified as police weapons.

Also, such a force would require strategic bases throughout the world. When Roosevelt and Stalin had discussed bases at Teheran, the President's feeling was that several areas around the world should be internationalized as bases for the use of the policemen. This might mean taking territory for such bases away from some states, with or without their consent. As the principle of recognizing the sovereignty of *all* states became paramount during the planning, this idea was dropped.

An international air force also presented practical problems. Who would command it? Who would supply the planes? A hodgepodge of planes from several nations would not make sense, and it seemed unlikely that any of the Big Three would consent to the exclusive use of another nation's planes. Finally, it was recognized that the United States Congress would probably never sign a blank check that would place American forces of any kind under foreign or international command.

After much discussion the planners decided to recommend the following alternative: supplying of contingents by all members, the actual members to be involved in each particular case to be determined by the Council. The pertinent paragraphs of the Tentative Proposals read, in part:

The member states should undertake to furnish forces and facilities when needed for this purpose at the call of the Executive Council and in accordance with a general agreement governing the number and type of forces and the kind and extent of facilities to be provided. . . . It should be a duty of the Executive Council to formulate as rapidly as possible plans and procedure for the negotiation of such agreement.

The idea of maintaining permanent internationalized bases was discarded. Instead the planners proposed:

The Executive Council should be empowered to call upon member states to grant rights of passage and to furnish facilities, including bases, necessary to the effective action of forces operating under authority of the council. The conditions of the exercise of these rights and of the furnishing of facilities, including bases, should be determined, in advance or at the time of action, by agreement between the Executive Council and the member states in whose territories these rights and facilities are required.

Related to the subject of enforcement was that of disarmament. Roosevelt's ideal had been that the small states, to whom armaments represented a great economic burden, should be totally disarmed. This was never seriously considered. In fact, in the early stages of planning, the word "disarmament" disappeared, to be replaced by the phrase "limitation of armaments," which in turn gave way to "regulation of armaments."

The initial thinking of the State Department planners was that the big powers should agree among themselves as to the extent of their armed forces and that other states should reduce their armed forces to the amount necessary for domestic policing and contingents for international use, this limitation to be determined by the Council. The trend of thinking soon departed from separate systems for small and large states and from the idea of an imposition of a limitation by the Council, which would be controlled by the large states. This was in line with the growing recognition of the rights and attitudes of the small states. The final proposal on this subject read:

In order to promote the establishment and maintenance of international security and peace with the least diversion of the world's human and economic resources for armaments, the Executive Council should be made responsible for initiating negotiations for the conclusion of a general international agreement . . . for the establishment of a system of regulation of armaments and armed forces.

Another point of discussion by the Agenda Group on which there was no uniformity of opinion was the size of and membership of the Council. Everybody agreed that the major powers should be permanent members and that there should be some small states represented, but how many and for how long was a subject of much debate. When the outline plan was submitted to Roosevelt he accepted the Council in lieu of the Four Policemen, but he wanted to hold the Council to seven members. However, most of the planners felt that the small states should have one more member than the large states. While the large states were the "Big Four" this meant at least nine members.

Majority membership by the small states would seem to make it possible for them to dominate the Council, and the decision to give them a majority was probably motivated by the psychological effect it would have on the small states. In practice, it was inconceivable that the small states would ever vote as a block against the big powers because, regardless of which small states were on the Council, at least one of them would surely be under the influence of the United States or Great Britain, and the continuance of Anglo-American agreement was taken for granted.

During the planning there were informal exchanges of views with Great Britain, which continued to stress that France should be considered, at least at some future time, as a major power. After the Anglo-American invasion of France the French Committee of National Liberation was recognized as the provisional government of France—albeit reluctantly by Roosevelt. Secretary Hull was willing to include France as a permanent member of the Council, but to this Roosevelt would not agree. His nomination for a fifth permanent member, if there was to be a fifth permanent member, was Brazil. The final recommendations in

the Tentative Proposal for membership on the Council
were:

The Executive Council should consist of eleven states mem-
bers of the international organization. These states should be
elected annually [this was later changed to biannually] by the
General Assembly and should not be immediately eligible for
re-election except that the United States of America, the
United Kingdom of Great Britain and Northern Ireland, the
Union of Soviet Socialist Republics, and the Republic of
China should have continuing tenure.

There should be a provision in the basic instrument that
whenever the Executive Council finds that a government
freely chosen by the French people has been established and
is in effective control of the territory of the French Republic,
France should be added to the list of states members having
continuing tenure on the Council.

One problem that was not solved by the State Department planners, and which would not finally be solved
until Roosevelt, Churchill, and Stalin met at Yalta, was the
question of voting in the Council. It was easy to agree that
all "procedural decisions"—routine matters—might be decided by a simple majority. But on any question involving
security the need for the large states to dominate the
Council was never questioned. The prevalent point of
view was that such decisions should be made by a majority
of the total membership that included all of the major
powers.

This matter of requiring unanimity by the major powers in all cases was wrangled over at great length by the
Agenda Group. There was a suggestion that some decisions
might be made by a majority which included three of the
four large states. It was recognized that the Senate would
never ratify a charter which contained such a provision as

applied to enforcement action. First, it would obligate the United States to the commitment of American troops upon the decision of representatives of foreign states. Whether or not the commitment was called a police action, in fact it might mean that American forces would be engaged in war; and the Constitution provides that only Congress can declare war. Also, there was concern that a majority of the Council might make decisions on what the United States considered domestic matters that were in its exclusive jurisdiction.

There was a possibility that the United States might not agree with the rest of the Council as to whether a certain matter was or was not domestic. As an obvious instance, suppose that the United States and Panama became involved in a dispute regarding the former's lease on the Canal Zone. Under a three-quarter rule of permanent member voting the Council might decide that this dispute was approaching a breach of the peace and propose to ettle it in favor of Panama. The United States would never agree that any decisions regarding the Panama Canal could be made without its approval. In general, although this was not directly expressed, the United States was inclined to feel that all matters in the Western Hemisphere were domestic. The Monroe Doctrine was no longer unilateral, but it was—and still is—a potent force in American foreign policy.

Those who briefly supported the three-quarter rule pointed out that if one of the big powers committed an act of aggression and the others, plus some small states, could not vote to take action against it, the peace-keeping organization was nothing more than a four power alliance. No state would vote for action against itself, so if a large state became an aggressor no action could be taken if the decision had to be unanimous. However, it was soon realized that enforcement action against a large state meant all-out war, probably World War III. In such a case, the peace-keeping organization would be out of business anyway, so they might as well agree on the need for unanimity. The Tentative Proposals on this point provided: "Decisions with respect to the following matters should be taken by a majority vote including the concurring votes of all member states having continuing tenure." Subsequently this was changed to a majority of seven members, including the five permanent members.

The "following matters" included "the assumption on its own initiative or on reference to it of jurisdiction over a dispute; the terms of settlement of disputes; the negotiations for a general agreement on the regulation of armaments and armed forces; the determination of threats to the peace, of breaches of the peace, and of acts obstructing measures for the maintenance of security and peace; and the institution and application of measures of enforcement."

All other decisions were to be made by a simple majority. The one exception to unanimity among the major powers in the Tentative Proposals was: "In all decisions any state member of the Executive Council should have the right to abstain from voting, but in such case the abstaining member should be bound by the decision." The Agenda Group had no specific suggestion as to what should be done if one of the major powers should become an aggressor. The Proposals merely provided: "Provisions will need to be worked out with respect to the voting procedure in the event of a dispute in which one or more of the members of the Council having continuing tenure are directly involved."

The provisions for unanimity of voting by the permanent members of the Security Council in the Charter of the United Nations led to what is called the "veto power." It is questionable whether "veto" is the best word to use in this instance, since the word usually denotes the negation of a legislative act by an executive. In this case it merely means an opposing vote by one member of a council. But regardless of what it is called there is a general impression that the veto power is in the Charter because of Russian insistence. This impression came about during the late 1940's and 1950's when the Russian representative on the Security Council vetoed practically everything that the body proposed to do. At times the Russian vetoes came almost daily.

Actually, as the Tentative Proposals indicate, the veto power is in the Charter at the insistence of the United States—not of Russia. Later there was dissension between Russia and the other powers as to whether the veto should be unlimited or whether there might be an absence of unanimity on such things as the subjects which the Council would consider and recommendations for peaceful settlements. But the United States never even considered membership in an international organization in which it would not have veto power on any proposed enforcement action.

The planning was well along before much attention was given to the settlement of disputes between states by means other than enforcement, but in their final form the Tentative Proposals contained an entire section on this. After providing that all states, whether or not they were members of the international organization, should be required "to settle disputes by none but peaceful means," the Proposals continued:

The parties to any dispute the continuance of which is likely to endanger international security or peace should be obligated, first of all, to seek a settlement by negotiation, mediation, conciliation, arbitration, reference to the international court of justice, or other peaceful means of their own choice.

Where feasible, regional or other arrangements should be employed to bring about adjustment or settlement of local or regional controversies.

If the parties fail to effect a settlement of such a dispute by the means above indicated, they should be obligated to refer it to the Executive Council.

In line with the principle of building up the authority of the Assembly, the Agenda Group sought to involve this organ in steps toward peaceful settlement and suggested that it should be empowered "to make, on its own initiative or on request of a member state, reports on and recommendations for the peaceful adjustment of any situation or controversy the continuation of which it deems likely to impair the general welfare" and "to assist the Executive Council, upon its request, in enlisting the cooperation of all states toward giving effect to action under consideration in or decided upon by the Council."

In short, either the Assembly or the Council could recommend a peaceful settlement. The recommendation was not obligatory, but if it was not accepted by a party to the dispute the Council might decide that the dispute represented a threat to the peace and take enforcement action.

This brought about discussion of another alternative for voting procedure in the Council. It was suggested that the veto power might not apply to a recommendation of a peaceful settlement; the Council could propose such a settlement without a unanimous vote of its permanent members. However, if the proposed settlement was not accepted and the question came up as to whether the dispute represented a breach of the peace, the dissenting or abstaining member would regain its veto power. In this case the veto would be limited to questions involving breaches of the peace and enforcement action.

The Agenda Group recognized that there must be some provision for regional organizations in the Charter of a general organization. One of the most severe criticisms of the Covenant of the League of Nations in the United States was that it did not have proper respect for the Monroe Doctrine. The American Congress would demand that a Pan-American organization should have preference over the general organization in settling matters in the Western Hemisphere. The Tentative Proposals provided:

The organization should be so constituted as to make possible the existence of regional organizations or other arrangements or policies not inconsistent with its purposes, and to enable such organizations and arrangements to function on their own initiation or by reference from the general organization on matters of security and peace which are appropriate for regional adjustment. The general organization should at all times be kept informed of the activities in matters of security and peace undertaken by regional organizations or under regional or other arrangements.

The Tentative Proposals contained other sections on the "General Character of an International Organization"; "A General Assembly"; "An International Court of Justice"; "Arrangements for Economic and Social Cooperation"; "General Administrations and Secretariat"; and "Procedure of Establishment and Inauguration." They also contained a title, "Arrangements for Territorial Trusteeships," but under this they merely said: *"Note:* Documents on this subject will be available later."

On May 30, 1944, Secretary Hull advised the ambassadors of Great Britain, Russia, and China that the United States was ready to proceed with diplomatic "conversations" about an international organization. The word "conversations" rather than "conference" was used to convince the small states that this meeting would be very informal and that nothing would be decided without them. It had already been agreed that the meeting would be held in Washington, D.C., and at some point a private estate called Dumbarton Oaks was selected as the specific site. The Russians objected to meeting with China, so it was agreed that the British and Americans would first meet with Russia and then have a separate meeting with China.

The British and the Chinese accepted the invitation from the United States immediately, the former suggesting that draft papers be exchanged before the meeting. It required three diplomatic communications to get an affirmative answer from the Russians, who at first said that they did not want to exchange papers; all they wanted to talk about was security and enforcement. However, when they received the American "Tentative Proposals for a General International Organization" they decided that they wanted more time to study them and would submit their own agenda paper. The British and Chinese memoranda in reply to the proposals of the United States generally endorsed them with minor questions. The brief Russian paper reiterated their opinion that the talks should be limited to a proposed organization devoted exclusively to security. They admitted that economic and social matters were important but felt that they might be handled by a separate international organization. They were obviously thinking in terms of a four power alliance rather than a United Nations, something like Roosevelt's original concept of the Four Policemen.

The Russian delay, their general attitude, and their refusal to make such things as Poland and the Baltic states matters of international consideration were annoying, to say the least. But Secretary Hull agreed with the President in his willingness to put up with a great deal from the Russians in order to secure their participation in the international organizaton. He later wrote:

I stressed the necessity for unity especially among the United States, Russia, and Great Britain, if this post-war international undertaking were to succeed. Malcontents in this country, I pointed out, were doing their best to drive Russia out of the international movement by constant attacks and criticisms largely about minor incidents or acts.

It was August 21 before the first, or Soviet, phase of the conversations started at Dumbarton Oaks. By this time American public opinion had switched from the isolationism of past years to hopeful expectancy, even enthusiasm, for an international organization. The matter had been lifted above the realm of politics when both parties agreed to keep it out of the 1944 election campaign. The State Department had ruled that the press would be excluded from working sessions and that news during the meeting would be limited to biweekly communiqués on "procedural" matters. This was rather naïve on the part of the planners. Washington press correspondents had such good contacts with some delegates that, with one exception, everything that happened at Dumbarton Oaks leaked to the press in time for the next morning's papers.

The Tentative Proposals was the only detailed and fully developed agenda paper and was accepted as the basis for discussion. Almost all matters were discussed in relation to the American suggestions. It is safe to say that the nucleus of what would become the Charter of the United Nations was this document prepared by the U.S. State Department with the help and advice of a committee of Senators, some private experts, and private organizations, and with the approval of and comments by Franklin Roosevelt.

All went well in the opening stages of the conversations. Russia proposed that the organization should be called "The International Security Organization," but was satisfied with the counter suggestion that security be emphasized by calling the Executive Council the "Security Council." The Soviets then proposed "World Union" for the title of the general organization. The Americans objected on the grounds that this sounded like some kind of a superstate. The others finally deferred to the American proposal of "The United Nations" as a title. The Americans also held out for the word "Charter" as the name of the document which would effectuate the United Nations because "from Magna Carta to the Atlantic Charter this term has meant liberty and freedom under law, which is the essence of this instrument." The Russians said that this word did not translate into their language as an alternative, but their objection was a mild one.

All agreed that the organization should be generally similar in format to the League of Nations, with a Council, an Assembly, a Secretariat, and a World Court. The Soviets at first held out for their idea of limiting it to security matters. The Anglo-American view was that the strongest organ would be the Security Council and that this would give the Russians what they wanted but would not limit the general organization to this area. The chief Soviet delegate, Andrei Gromyko, secured permission from Moscow to agree to this. All four nations favored an Assembly in which each of the United Nations would be represented, but the United States took the lead in trying to make this organ something more than the debating society which it had been in the League.

The United States wanted to assure that the Charter would make some reference to human rights and proposed a clause to this effect. Both Great Britain and Russia disagreed with the wording suggested by the United States. The American group was stubborn on this, and cables flew between Washington and London and Moscow before permission was obtained to include a statement that:

With a view to the creation of conditions of stability and well-being, which are necessary for peaceful and friendly relations among nations, the Organization should facilitate solutions of international economic, social and other humanitarian problems and promote respect for human rights and fundamental freedoms.

The American proposal for an Economic and Social Council under the General Assembly was accepted; none of the other nations had any reference to this subject in their papers.

All four governments agreed that there should be a Secretariat to handle administrative machinery and provide technical experts in various fields and that there should be a chief administrative executive—a Secretary General. The details of this aspect were left rather vague, as were those on the World Court. There was some talk as to whether this should be a new organization or the old court warmed over, but it was decided to leave this to a committee of jurists who were to meet later.

The first rift in the amicable atmosphere came on the subject of membership. It was agreed that all members of the wartime United Nations should be initial members and that other "peace-loving" states should be admitted. The enemy states would not be eligible for membership, at least until they reformed. Then Gromyko exploded a bombshell by demanding that each of the sixteen Soviet republics should be an individual member.

Secretary Hull was "amazed" at this proposal and later wrote, "no such question had ever entered the minds of any of us . . . who had been working in post-war planning." F.D.R. said the idea was "absurd" and told Under Secretary of State Edward Stettinius (who had replaced Sumner Welles and was leading the United States delegation) to tell Gromyko that it would be just as logical for the United States to demand forty-eight memberships, one for each state. Fearing the effect of this proposal on American public opinion Roosevelt ordered that it be kept as quiet as possible; in Hull's words it might "blow off the roof." Within the American delegation it was referred to as the "X matter," and it was the only aspect of the meeting that did not leak to the press.

Although the Russian demand for individual memberships for each state in the U.S.S.R. seems ridiculous, it must be recognized that the Soviet leaders could not believe the other American republics were truly independent of the United States or that the Dominions within the British Commonwealth had sufficient freedom to vote against the mother country. In their thinking it was inconceivable that strong states would permit such latitude to their "satellites." They firmly believed that Great Britain and the United States would control large blocks of votes in the assembly, so Russia should be similarly favored. Also, there is reason to believe that Gromyko's proposal was made at least partly for its local political effect at home.

When Hull endeavored to induce Gromyko to withdraw the proposal the Russian replied that his country would not participate in a formal conference on the United Nations unless it was agreed to. In an exchange of cables between Roosevelt and Stalin the Russian dictator pointed out that "the Ukraine and Byelorussia . . . are greater in population and political importance than certain other countries which we all agree should belong to the . . . initiators of the . . . International Organization." He did agree that it was a matter which they might discuss later.

Because the failure of the Dumbarton Oaks Conversations might preclude the formation of an international organization, or at least its indefinite postponement, the United States was eager that they should not fail. It was therefore decided that the proposal for membership, and certain other matters, would be considered as "open questions" to be decided by the heads of state or at the later, formal conference. The Dumbarton Oaks Conversations could terminate—with seeming success—and still leave these things up in the air. On the subject of membership

the Dumbarton Oaks proposals merely said, "Membership
of the Organization should be open to all peace-loving
states."

The other important issue that became an open question was the matter of the veto. The records indicate that
there seemed to be some confusion among the American
delegates as to their official position. They were in favor
of a veto, but with some limitations. Hull later wrote:
"There was still some difference of opinion among us,
however, as to whether this abstention from voting should
apply only to the pacific settlement of disputes in which
one or more of the major nations were involved, or should
apply also to enforcement action." As to the general
United States' attitude toward the veto Hull further
wrote:

> In all the discussions with my associates in post-war plan-
> ning, two important conditions had been understood and
> repeatedly stated in connection with the veto. The first was
> that none of the permanent members of the Council would
> exercise its right of veto capriciously or arbitrarily. It would
> call this power forth only on a matter of the gravest concern to
> itself, never on secondary matters and never in a way to pre-
> vent thorough discussion of any issue. . . . The second condi-
> tion was that we were thinking largely of the application of
> the veto power to military or other means of compulsion.

The British view was that a permanent member of the
Security Council should not have the right to veto a matter
in which it was a principal, except in the case of enforcement action. Such things as the use of the veto in connection with what matters the Council might consider, in connection with peaceful settlements, and in relation to domestic jurisdiction were never considered in detail. Before

the conversations reached this point the Soviets took the stand the veto power must be unlimited—and from this they would not budge.

Roosevelt again cabled Stalin on this, saying, in effect, "We and the British both feel strongly that in the decisions of the Council, parties to a dispute should not vote even if one of the members is a permanent member of the Council; I know public opinion in the United States would never understand or support a plan of international organization which violated this principle." Stalin replied that he understood that Churchill and Roosevelt had agreed to the principle of complete unanimity at Teheran —which they had, to the extent to which it was discussed. He further stated that the Soviet Union would never agree to any limitation of the veto in any matter which might involve its security.

The Russian position was perhaps best explained by a memorandum from Averill Harriman, United States ambassador at Moscow:

We had sufficient evidence to foresee that, if a world organization were established, requiring agreement of all permanent members for the consideration of any dispute, regardless of whether or not one of them was involved, the Soviet Government would ruthlessly block consideration by the Council of any question that it considered affected its interest. The Soviet Union would also insist that such a matter be settled by the Soviet Union with the other country . . . involved, particularly any dispute with her neighbors.

There were some within the American delegation who were willing to accept the Russian point of view in order to prevent the conversations from collapsing. Their memorandum on this point concluded:

If we closely examine from a realistic point of view, this question which threatens to wreck the organization before it has started, it would seem that this question of veto or no veto will NOT be an essential factor in determining the future success of the organization. A great power when dealing with matters vital to it will not accede to the dictates of the organization whether or not it has a veto, and in such case the organization, as regards the great powers, will be equally impotent to enforce its decision.

However, the delegation finally decided that the matter must be "reserved for discussion at a higher level," that is, by the heads of state. Their memorandum on this said:

A quick compromise now on the Russian terms might conceivably imperil the success of the organization. It might be rejected by the Dominions, the Latin American republics, and other states. The very quickness of our decision might make them feel that we had too readily sold them down the river.

The whole subject was finally covered in the Dumbarton Oaks Proposals by this statement: "Note: The question of voting procedure in the Security Council is still under consideration."

Shortly after they were made public the Dumbarton Oaks Proposals were subjected to a confidential analysis by the Yale Institute of International Studies. Some of their comments are of interest in conveying an understanding of where the concept of the new international organizations stood after these conversations. The institute pointed out that the United Nations was not

. . . a universal organization or a legal system binding on all states. No state will be obliged to enter. In this respect the announced principle of "sovereign equality" is given full play. . . . Nothing in the way of understanding will be gained by likening the United Nations to a super-state. To attribute to it legislative, executive, or even judicial powers will be more misleading than enlightening.

The organization would have but limited judicial power through an international court of justice. In this court, said the institute:

. . . the great powers who are the permanent members of the Security Council will in all likelihood have a veto; and this means that at least as far as they are concerned the court's jurisdiction will depend, as that of the Permanent Court of International Justice has depended, on voluntary submission. If this is so, another essential difference from the structure of states becomes apparent. One of the basic conditions on which order, justice, and equality depend within the state will be lacking in the international organization.

After stating that the Security Council was the "most vigorous and authoritative organ of the United Nations," the report continued:

The Council's jurisdiction in disputes seems on the text to be independent of the parties' consent. But one capacious loophole has been left. The Council cannot touch a dispute arising out of a matter which by international law is solely within the domestic jurisdiction of a state.

When a state asserts that a claim advanced against it arises out of a matter solely within its domestic jurisdiction, who will decide this question? Any threat or use of force in connection with the dispute might be regarded as lifting the matter out of the domestic category and so giving the Security Council jurisdiction. . . . Obviously so important a matter ought not to be left to controversial influence. . . .

The Security Council has no means of execution under its direct and immediate command. In the portion of the text dealing with diplomatic and economic sanctions, this is quite clear. The Council "calls upon" member states to take the necessary measures. . . .

In the still more serious case of military sanctions, the text is not so clear. At first glance it may be thought to give direct command over the . . . contingents which members are to hold immediately available for "combined international enforcement action." But these contingents, like any other armed forces provided by the members, are to be handled in accordance with special agreements to be concluded among the members. In the absence of specific clauses . . . they will be brought into action through the national military authorities. . . .

The Security Council will not be an executive body whose orders are the sole authority necessary for economic and military action. Its orders must be channeled through national authorities, and it cannot punish or replace officials who refuse to act.

The institute analysis had a long section on the pros and cons of permanent member voting unanimity in the Security Council and introduced one new thought relative to the small states:

The small states may insist upon [complete] unanimity in the Security Council of the new organization. If they do, they will reduce that body to the helplessness of the Council of the League. Important decisions will then be made by the great powers without reference to the Council, and the small states will lose all means of influencing them. Alternatively, they may take the stand that no organization at all will be better than the legal admission of inequality and the acceptance of a system which cannot be made to work against members of the inner coalition, and which will therefore offer them no guaranteed protection against great-power usurpations. . . .

The proposed organization will not lessen any existing protection which the small states have against the great. No charter is required to put the great powers on top of the heap. They are there already. That is the situation in fact. As for the situation in law, the very rule of unanimity among the permanent members of the Security Council will tend to prevent the use of the organization in any oppressive manner. Most small powers will find at least one friend among the permanent members. Moreover, if they vote together, the small states can veto action by the Council.

Under the title "Armaments" the institute report said, in part:

The regulation and reduction of armaments receive scanty attention in our text. . . . We are told that the Military Staff Committee will have among its functions that of advising and assisting the Security Council in all questions relating "to the regulation of armaments, and to possible disarmament." The modesty and the tentativeness of this clause touching what ranked before the war as one of the major problems of international politics indicate very clearly a new orientation. . . .

It has sometimes been argued that one important reason for giving each of the great powers a veto, and thus ensuring that the organization cannot be turned against any of them, is that they would otherwise be unwilling to exchange information on forces and equipment. Against this must be set the possibility that, since the organization cannot protect the great powers against one another, they will seek reinsurance in the development of superior armed forces. It is, after all, a common habit of governments to formulate "multiple-contingency" policies. Only quite extraordinary confidence in the United Nations will make them cease planning for the eventuality of its failure. This being so, we should be optimistic indeed to count on full and frank exchange of military information between the Soviet Union, the United States, and Great Britain, whatever the voting arrangements may be in the Security Council.

Under the heading "Dependent Peoples":

The Dumbarton Oaks text does not touch the large and inevitable problem of dependent peoples. . . . Eventually, the

Security Council and the Economic and Social Council must be empowered to concern themselves in some measure with the military use and the general development of colonial and mandated territories. There is, however, a preliminary stage, namely, that of fixing the terms of peace.

The Yale Institute felt that the Dumbarton Oaks Proposals did not

. . . differ so broadly from the League of Nations as some commentators appear to believe. . . . The principal difference lies in the machinery. . . . The Dumbarton Oaks text proposes an Economic and Social Council. Through this instrument the General Assembly is to discharge its responsibility of promoting "respect for human rights and fundamental freedoms" and of facilitating "solutions of international economic, social and other humanitarian problems." . . .

In all this large division of the United Nations' work, there is complete formal equality of great and small states. This is possible because . . . [the] Economic and Social Council . . . will have no power to make decisions calling for obligatory action by members.

The report pointed out that, unlike the League of Nations, there was not provision for a state to withdraw from the United Nations. "What the states are being invited to do, in other words, is to accept, of their own free and equal will, permanent obligations. It will be a breach of obligation and an illegal act for them to withdraw."

The report commended proposals for "Regional Arrangements." "These," it said, "have distinct merits. Regional association is probably an irresistible tendency. If so it should be canalized and disciplined rather than resisted."

Under the heading "Transitional Arrangements" the Dumbarton Oaks Proposals ended by stating: "No provision of the Charter should preclude action taken or authorized in relation to enemy states as a result of the present war by the Governments having responsibility for such action." This, the Yale Institute analysis said,

. . . may be interpreted as a warning to the forthcoming drafting conference [of the United Nations] that the terms of peace with the Axis states will lie outside its province. . . .

The principal Allied belligerents may constitute themselves a continuing body for the exclusive enforcement of the peace terms. But their success or failure in keeping Germany and Japan disarmed, and in controlling the industries of those countries with a view either to restricting military potential or to reparations in kind, will affect the fortunes of a great many nations. The United Nations will not be able to stand aloof from the results. No general organization for security or welfare could avoid being involved in the consequences of such a war as this has been. If those consequences continue to disturb the relations of states, the United Nations will ultimately be held responsible.

In its summary the Yale Institute report said:

The plan itself is not Utopian. . . . It will not satisfy the demand that the war has stimulated in many quarters for radically new departures in political organization. It does not echo the higher notes of idealism struck by some foremost political leaders in their promises of a new world. But it does prepare the way for a fresh start on the path towards more lasting peace. This may prove to be a better beginning than the League of Nations.

The summary ended with what has proved to be a uniquely accurate prophecy:

Our organization provides no compulsory or dependable machinery for settling disputes or keeping the peace between the greatest states. In other words, it does not contain in itself the essential conditions of its own survival. It can only operate in the absence of serious conflicts of interest between the per-

manent members of the proposed Security Council. The
avoidance or solution of such conflicts will depend on constant
good will. The greatest risk to which the organization will be
exposed is that the governments and peoples of the United
States, Britain, and the Soviet Union, having once set it up,
may regard the maintenance of a rather delicate mechanism as
their sole duty to peace. So doing, they may fail in the
perpetual vigilance and wisdom which alone can keep them in
harmony.

6

On to Yalta

At the termination of the Dumbarton Oaks Conversations the President sounded a note of cautious optimism. He referred to the forthcoming United Nations Organization as a "great objective," but, he said, "We don't know if it is going to work. It doesn't guarantee peace forever, but we hope at least it will guarantee world peace while any of us today are still alive. That will be something."

In general the Dumbarton Oaks Proposals were well received in the United States. Everyone seemed to agree that proposing something definite in connection with establishing an international organization was a step in the right direction. But there were some doubts about the actual organization that was proposed. Some of these were expressed in a formal statement by the Federal Council of the Churches. After saying, "The Dumbarton Oaks Proposals initiate a definite plan for the continuing collaboration of the United Nations and in due course other nations. The Federal Council of Churches has long sought such a step and welcomes its occurrence," the Council's statement continued:

We recognize that transition from international anarchy to a complete constitutional world order cannot occur at a single step. It was thus to be expected that any presently practicable plan should fall short of what will be required to assure lasting peace. The organization proposed has many of the characteristics of a military alliance of a few great powers. Certain provisions seem to envisage a division of the world into regional spheres of influence dominated by one or another of the great powers. Reliance is placed primarily on force unrelated to any explicitly agreed upon principles of justice. Further, the proposed organization should be more adequately endowed with curative functions needed to deal with the causes of war and with creative functions needed to draw the nations together in fellowship.

At the same meeting of the Federal Council of Churches, John Foster Dulles, who would become President Eisenhower's Secretary of State, made the point that the United States was denying its own ideals by its failure to support them in opposition to its allies. He said:

We are hesitant about giving or accepting collaboration with reference to the hard problems that daily present themselves. We like collaboration as an idea. We fear it as a reality. In consequence, there has developed a sort of tacit understanding with our principal allies. They will give us world cooperation on paper—which is the way we like it. In return, we will drop out of the actual practice of collaboration, leaving each a free hand in its area of special interest.

These fears stemmed from the situation in Europe at the end of 1944. Russia had concluded a bilateral armistice with Roumania, without consulting its allies, and was paying only lip service to Anglo-American efforts to have some say in armistice terms for Hungary and Bulgaria. Churchill's fears had been well founded; Stalin intended to keep under Soviet influence all territory that had been "liberated" from German influence by Russian troops. The Russians considered relations with their neighbors as domestic matters in which the United Nations would have no jurisdiction.

In the minds of many Americans, Great Britain's skirts were not spotless in this respect. The British were supporting what were considered reactionary governments in exile for several countries. Such governments would bring their countries within the British sphere of influence. This was true in Greece, where the British dominated the situation as the Russians did elsewhere in the Balkans. Their ideas for a new government in conquered Italy were also suspect.

It was obvious that so far as the immediate postwar Europe was concerned, Russia—and to a lesser extent Britain—was not planning to conform in practice to some of the principles of the Atlantic Charter in participating in a new international order. They were playing the old game of power politics. There was no talk of self-determination, plebiscites, or even temporary trusteeship for any of the peoples involved.

The American government was concerned about what was happening, but did not take a strong position on it. The U.S. State Department did propose the formation of a Provisional Security Council composed of the Big Three and France "to supervise the re-establishment of popular government and the maintenance of order in the liberated

states in Europe and in the German satellite states, pending the establishment of the United Nations." In any case
of "doubt concerning the status of the government" in a
liberated country or in a satellite, "the proposed council
could investigate and require in such a case the establishment of a coalition government, broadly representative of
all elements in the population" and "constituted under
the direct supervision of the Council or a panel of special
observers representing each of the four countries." The
State Department memorandum pointed out that American influence must be exerted so that "democratic groups
in the liberated countries would 'be left free to determine'
and to participate in their interim governments." If this
were not done, "it might later be impossible 'to establish
permanent democratic regimes based on the four freedoms.' " However, no effective influence was exerted by
the United States, and nothing came of the State Department proposal.

Roosevelt sought to justify the position of the United
States government in his Annual Message to Congress in
January, 1945. He said: "We have seen already, in areas
liberated from the Nazi and Fascist tyranny, what problems peace will bring. And we delude ourselves if we attempt to believe wishfully that all these problems can be
solved overnight." In the future, he claimed, "the misuse
of power, as implied in the term 'power-politics,' must not
be a controlling factor in international relations." But it
would be wrong to insist on our own solution to every
immediate problem. He stressed the idea that "Perfection-
ism, no less than isolationism or imperialism or power-
politics, may obstruct the paths of international peace. Let
us not forget that the retreat to isolationism a quarter of a

century ago was started not by a direct attack against international cooperation, but against the alleged imperfections of the peace."

He pledged the United States to use its influence "to secure so far as it is humanly possible, the fulfillment of the principles of the Atlantic Charter," but added:

> I do not wish to give the impression that all mistakes can be avoided and that many disappointments are not inevitable in the making of peace. But we must not this time lose the hope of establishing an international order which will be capable of maintaining peace and realizing through the years more perfect justice between nations. To do this we must be on our guard not to exploit and exaggerate the differences between us and our allies.

This is Roosevelt the pragmatist talking. It is easy for the Monday morning quarterback to label his thinking shallow, but war was still raging in Europe, and in the minds of the American people the important immediate objective was to end it with the loss of as few American lives as possible. Every military leader agreed that this required the good will of Russia. And, at that point, it is doubtful that the United States *could* have exerted much influence on Russia. If that opportunity ever existed it was lost after the Russian military steamroller gained momentum. Secretary Hull later wrote:

> A suggestion was advanced from time to time that all we had to do to bring about a settlement was to threaten Russia that we would cut off . . . Lend-lease assistance. . . . Neither the President nor I seriously entertained this suggestion for a moment. Russia, Britain, and the United States were in the same boat. . . . Our Lend-lease supplies . . . were helping to . . . eliminate enemy armed forces on the Eastern Front

which otherwise we would have had to fight on the Western Front. . . .

If we made the threat and Russia still refused to accede to our demands, we would then have faced a dilemma. Would we cut off military aid and thereby hurt ourselves militarily? Or would we continue it, thereby proving that our threat had been an empty one? And if we did cut it off, and let Moscow go its own way, could we then have the slightest hope of reaching a general post-war agreement with the Soviet Government?

During 1944 Roosevelt had been pressing for another meeting with Churchill and Stalin. As usual, the Russian dictator was evasive. By the time the Dumbarton Oaks Conversations ended in October it was a month before the national election, and the President could not leave the country then or until after his inauguration in January, 1945. Stalin finally agreed to a meeting in February, but only if it was held on Russian soil, and he proposed Yalta in the Crimea. Roosevelt's protestations that he could not go so far away were in vain. This time the Russian dictator pleaded "doctor's orders" rather than military necessity for his insistence on staying close to home.

In their cables regarding this meeting Roosevelt told Churchill that he did not want to stay in Yalta more than five or six days. The Prime Minister proposed that, in that event, the two of them and their military men should hold a previous conference in Malta. He jestingly added, "I do not see any other way of realizing our hopes about World Organization in five or six days. Even the Almighty took seven."

As soon as agreement was reached for another Big Three meeting the State Department started to prepare briefing material for the President. The principal nonmilitary problem was the voting procedure in the Security Council. The State Department was firm in its conviction that the United States could not yield to Russia on this. Their memorandum to Roosevelt said:

Our talks with members of Congress and with many individuals and groups throughout the country clearly indicate that failure to provide for modification of the unanimity rule would . . . become a powerful weapon in the hands of both the perfectionists and isolationists. Moreover, acceptance by us of a straight unanimity rule would inevitably be interpreted as surrender to Russia. These factors might well jeopardize our chances for adequate public and Congressional support in this country. At the same time, our discussions with representatives of the American Republics and of other United Nations have already disclosed their strong opposition to the straight unanimity rule.

As late as December, 1944, the President seemed to be in complete agreement on this.

If the Russians proved adamant at Yalta the State Department offered the President three lines of retreat. "First, all pacific-settlement functions might be transferred to the General Assembly, leaving the Council with only enforcement functions." In this case the United States could agree to unlimited unanimity in the Security Council. Second, the Dumbarton Oaks Proposals might be scrapped and a new conference held to plan an organization of a different structure, based on an unlimited veto, but probably without enforcement authority. It was admitted that such an organization would be nothing more than a consultative institution, and probably ineffective, but the point might be used as a bargaining position. Third, it was suggested as a last resort that an unlimited veto might be accepted for a definite limited period, perhaps five years.

This was proposed only as a last ditch alternative to not having any postwar organization.

A month before the Yalta meeting the President gave indications that he was weakening on the veto question. He intimated that the Soviet position on unanimity might not be wholly a bad one and that the point might be used to bargain with the Soviets on the question of votes for its sixteen republics.

During the discussion of the veto at this time the State Department sought to clarify the position of the United States by sending a memorandum to Russia and Great Britain on its concept of all the functions of the Security Council. This is included here in full to clarify the picture as of this time. In the United States' opinion the Security Council powers would include:

   I. Recommendations to the General Assembly on
     1. Admission of new members;
     2. Suspension of a member;
     3. Expulsion of a member;
     4. Election of the Secretary General.
  II. Restoration of the rights and privileges of a suspended member.
III. Promotion of peaceful settlement of disputes, including the following questions:
     1. Whether a dispute or a situation brought to the Council's attention is of such a nature that its continuation is likely to threaten the peace;
     2. Whether the Council should call on the parties to settle or adjust the dispute or situation by means of their own choice;
     3. Whether the Council should make a recommendation to the parties as to methods and procedures of settlement;
     4. Whether the legal aspects of the matter before it

should be referred by the Council for advice to the International Court of Justice;

5. Whether, if there exists a regional agency for peaceful settlement of local disputes, such an agency should be asked to concern itself with the controversy.

IV. Removal of threats to the peace and suppression of breaches of the peace, including the following questions:

1. Whether failure on the part of the parties to a dispute to settle it by means of their own choice, or accordance with the recommendations of the Security Council, in fact constitutes a threat to the peace;

2. Whether any other actions on the part of any country constitute a threat to the peace or a breach of the peace;

3. What measures should be taken by the Council to maintain or restore the peace and the manner in which such measures should be carried out;

4. Whether a regional agency should be authorized to take measures of enforcement.

V. Approval of special agreement or agreements for the provision of armed forces and facilities.

VI. Formulation of plans for a general system of regulation of armaments and submission of such plans to the member states.

VII. Determination of whether the nature and the activities of a regional agency or arrangement for the maintenance of peace and security are consistent with the purposes and principles of the general Organization.

A decision by the Council would require the vote of seven members, including all five permanent members, in all matters except those in category III. In this category a permanent member who was a party to a dispute would not vote, and unanimity would not be required.

The main concern at Yalta was a military matter—getting a positive commitment from Stalin to bring Russia

into the war against Japan. Related to this was the political
situation in China. The Nationalist government of Chiang
Kai-shek, headquartered at Chungking, had been fighting
the Chinese Communists longer than they had been fighting the Japanese. Now, both Communists and Nationalists
were fighting the Japanese, but independently. Chiang was
rabidly anticommunist and would not share Lend-lease
armaments with them. He also, according to American
military men, was holding back some of his forces from the
conflict with the Japanese to use against his older internal
enemy if necessary.

The United States was pressuring Chiang to form a coalition government with the Communists. This, it was believed, would relieve inner tensions, assure full Chinese
support in the war effort, and create a government with
which Russia could be friendly because of its Communist
element. Roosevelt's attitude toward communism is expressed in a statement that he made to Stalin to the effect
that he thought progress was being made toward bringing
the Nationalists and the Communists together, and that
"the fault lay more with the Chungking government than
with the so-called Communists." Later events would prove
that there was nothing "so called" about Chinese communism. The United States finally forced Chiang to accept
the Communists into his government by threatening to cut
off all postwar aid. It is ironic that the first big outside assist that the Communists received in taking over China
was from the United States.

At the time of Yalta the United States military leaders
estimated that the war with Japan would last for eighteen
months after the collapse of Germany, which was immi-
nent. It was therefore vital to get Russia into the war to

contain Japanese troops in Manchuria and North Korea while Americans invaded their homeland and to get air bases in Siberia from which American and Russian planes could bomb Japan. Roosevelt, and a very few others, knew that the top secret Manhattan Project was coming to fruition and would soon produce the atom bomb, two of which would end the war with Japan. But nobody knew, then, how powerful this new engine of destruction would be. It was thought that one atom bomb might be equal in force to all the conventional bombs which could be carried by a single flight of bombers, which would not make it a decisive weapon.

At Yalta, Stalin promised to bring Russia into the Japanese war within two or three months after Hitler was defeated—if the Russian terms were met. These terms included an Anglo-American guarantee that Russia would receive the Chinese cities of Port Arthur, for a naval base, and Darien, for a warm-water port. They also wanted the Japanese mandated Kurile Islands and Southern Sakhalin and control of the Manchurian railroads which connected Darien with the Russian homeland. Roosevelt and Stalin discussed these demands privately; and with minor and meaningless modifications, the President agreed to them. A formal statement to this effect was signed by the President and the Prime Minister. Although there was a clause that China would have to agree, it was decided to keep the agreement secret from Chiang until Stalin gave the word, on the grounds that it might leak to Japan before the Russians were ready to attack.

This was another, and extreme, case of expediency overruling idealism. The United Nations would not be involved in this switch of territory from China and Japan to

Russia, and self-determination or international trusteeship was never mentioned.

The other important political and territorial matter which was finally decided at Yalta was the future of Poland. This, too, was settled entirely on Russian terms, although there were some face-saving words in the agreement—which turned out to be meaningless. After breaking with the Polish government in exile, Russia had recognized a Communist government in Poland—the Lublin government. They now agreed that this would be broadened by the addition of "some" non-Communist Poles to form a provisional government, which would hold elections as soon as possible. They firmly refused to have these elections supervised by outsiders on the fanciful grounds that the Poles would be offended. They also refused to give up the half of Poland they had grabbed in 1939, but agreed that Poland could have some German territory in compensation.

There were three questions relative to the United Nations which had to be settled at Yalta before a formal organization conference could be held: First, voting procedure in the Security Council. Second, who would be the initial members? Third, should the proposed Charter provide for any kind of territorial trusteeship?

The main point of difference between Russia and the United States on voting procedure had to do with non-unanimity in cases of peaceful settlements of disputes. Under the Russian position a veto might block even discussion of a matter by the Security Council. Before Yalta, Stalin had told Ambassador Harriman that unless there was unanimity in the discussion of a peaceful settlement any further action to enforce a decision would probably be impossible. He said, "The principle of unity of action must be preserved from the inception of any dispute, it must never be diminished, and there must be no exceptions to it; otherwise, the entire organization would be emasculated."

There was some difference of opinion within the British and American governments as to the importance of the voting procedure matter. The U.S. State Department and the British Foreign Office insisted that limitation of the veto was crucial to the success of the international organization. Roosevelt and Churchill agreed that this was highly desirable, but at one time or another each indicated that he might give way to the Russian view.

At Yalta, Stalin at first pursued the reasoning which he had advanced to Harriman, saying, "the main thing was to prevent quarrels in the future between the three Great Powers and that the task, therefore, was to secure their unity for the future. The covenant of the new World Organization should have this as its primary task." He recalled that, in 1939, the shooting dispute between Russia and Finland had led to the expulsion of the Soviet Union from the League of Nations, an action instigated by Great Britain and France. He did not want to again put his country in a position where the other major powers could gang up against it. Churchill replied that he saw the force of that argument, but he did not believe that the world organization would eliminate disputes between powers and that would remain the function of diplomacy.

Roosevelt added: "Should there unfortunately be any differences between the Great Powers, and there might well be, this fact would become fully known to the world no matter what voting procedure was adopted." In any event, there was no method of preventing discussions of differences in the Assembly. He said that "full and friendly discussions in the Council would in no sense promote disunity, but on the contrary, would serve to demonstrate the confidence which the Great Powers had in each other and in the justice of their own policies."

The day after this discussion among the Big Three, Soviet Foreign Minister Molotov astonished everybody by quietly saying that the Russians now understood the American proposal for the first time and no longer objected to it.

In passing it might be remarked that the American proposal, as contained in the memorandum on Security Council powers which the State Department had sent to Great Britain and Russia, was far from the last word on this thorny subject. This memorandum left many things up in the air. It did not define "procedural" nor "substantive" matters. It said nothing about the veto in relation to matters of domestic jurisdiction. It had but a vague reference to the veto in relation to the actions of regional agencies. There would be millions of words said and written on all of these subjects before the matter was finally settled.

In the same statement in which he accepted the American proposal on the voting procedure, Molotov made a new, much modified, request on the acceptance of individual Soviet republics as initial members of the United Nations. The Russians now wanted three, or at least two, of their republics so treated: the Ukraine, White Russia, and Lithuania. The Soviet position was that these states had a similar relationship to the U.S.S.R. as some of the British Dominions had with their mother country.

Roosevelt had previously ridiculed the idea of Russia

having more than one membership in the Assembly. Now he at first tried to avoid a commitment and suggested that the matter be put on the agenda of the formal conference. Churchill concurred, although he would not oppose the Russian demand for fear that they would challenge the right of Canada, Australia, New Zealand, India, and the Union of South Africa to memberships. Then, Roosevelt suddenly about-faced and agreed, in essence, to the Ukraine and White Russia as members. The sense of agreement was that the United States and Great Britain would recommend the acceptance of the Russian request for membership for these two Soviet republics at the formal conference. The President could not agree to the inclusion of Lithuania as a Soviet republic because the United States still recognized a minister in Washington appointed by the prewar Lithuanian government.

Roosevelt's agreement on this caused some consternation on the part of political advisers in the American delegation. Ed Flynn, boss of New York's Tammany Hall, shuddered at the probable reaction of Irish voters in the big East Coast cities to an arrangement whereby Great Britain had six votes and Russia three votes to one vote for the United States. The President then wrote a letter to Stalin explaining that he might have to ask for three memberships for the United States in order to placate Congress and American public opinion. Both Stalin and Churchill promised to agree to this if necessary.

There were other details as to membership at the formal United Nations Conference. Both the United States and Russia wanted to limit attendance to those states which had declared war on one or more of the Axis countries and were thus already members of the United Nations. But

Roosevelt also wanted to find a way to secure admittance to six Latin American republics which had broken relations but not declared war. Churchill also wanted to get Egypt, Saudi Arabia, and Turkey in on the grounds that they had contributed much to the war effort as nonbelligerents. It was finally decided that these associated states would be given until March 1 to declare war and thus become eligible for admission to the United Nations.

The final problem was trusteeship, which had been ignored at Dumbarton Oaks. There was some difference of opinion on this among the Americans. Roosevelt was still strong for international trusteeships for mandated areas, certain territory that would be taken away from the Axis powers, and some colonial people. He and Stalin talked at length about trusteeship for Korea under the supervision of the Big Four.

American military leaders were much less enthusiastic about trusteeship. In Europe they wanted to avoid direct American participation in territorial questions because this might interfere with military cooperation. In the Pacific, the War Department wanted no general agreement on trusteeships which might limit the action of the United States in acquiring some of the Japanese mandated islands as American bases. In a memorandum on the subject, Secretary of War Stimson wrote:

Acquisition of them by the United States does not represent an attempt at colonization or exploitation. Instead, it is merely the acquisition by the United States of the necessary bases for the defense of the security of the Pacific for the future world. To serve such a purpose they must belong to the United States with absolute power to rule and fortify them. They are not colonies; they are outposts, and their acquisition is appropriate under the general doctrine of self-defense by the power which guarantees the safety of that area of the world.

Despite this internal difference, the State Department proposed at Yalta that conferences be held to provide "machinery in the World Charter for dealing with territorial trusteeship and dependent areas." At this, wrote Secretary of State Stettinius (who by now had replaced ailing Cordell Hull), "the Prime Minister exploded." Churchill angrily said that "he did not agree with one single word of this report on trusteeships." He would never listen to any proposal "that the British Empire is to be put into the dock and examined by everybody," and that he "would never yield one scrap of their heritage."

Stettinius explained that the reference to dependent territories applied only to those taken from the enemy, not to British colonies. Churchill insisted that this be spelled out and the State Department paper was revised to limit the proposal for territorial trusteeship to existing mandates of the League, territories detached from the enemy, and other territory which might "voluntarily" be placed under trusteeship. At Churchill's insistence it was also agreed that there would be no discussion of actual territories at the United Nations Conference. This final decision was more or less in line with the position of American military leaders.

With all of these things out of the way it was easily agreed that the United Nations Conference would be held in San Francisco about April 25, 1945. Invitations would be issued in the names of the permanent members of the Security Council and would "suggest" that the Dumbarton Oaks Proposals, as supplemented at Yalta, should be considered as "affording a basis for" the character of a general organization for the maintenance of international peace.

From the conference at Yalta the Big Three issued a "Declaration on Liberated Europe" for consumption at home and by the people of Europe. It said, in part:

The establishment of order in Europe and the re-building of national economic life must be achieved by processes which will enable the liberated peoples to destroy the last vestiges of Nazism and Fascism and to create democratic institutions of their own choice. This is a principle of the Atlantic Charter— the right of all peoples to choose the form of government under which they will live—the restoration of sovereign rights and self-government to those peoples who have been forcibly deprived of them by the aggressor nations. . . .

By this declaration we re-affirm our faith in the principles of the Atlantic Charter, our pledge in the Declaration by the United Nations, and our determination to build in coopera- tion with other peace-loving nations world order under law, dedicated to peace, security, freedom and general well-being of all mankind.

A communiqué was also issued from Yalta which said:

Our meeting here in the Crimea has re-affirmed our com- mon determination to maintain and to strengthen in the peace to come that unity of purpose and of action which has made victory possible and certain for the United Nations in this war. We believe that this is a sacred obligation which our Governments owe to our peoples and to all the peoples of the world.

Only with the continuing and growing cooperation and understanding among our three countries and among all the peace-loving nations can the highest aspiration of humanity be realized—a secure and lasting peace which will, in the words of the Atlantic Charter, "afford assurance that all the men in all the lands may live out their lives in freedom from fear and want."

It was obvious that the glowing words and promises of these documents were belied by the actual performance at Yalta. In both the Polish and Far Eastern deals there was no assurance that the people involved would have the right to "choose the form of government under which they would live." This was supposed to happen in Poland, but the history of the Baltic states was reasonably conclusive evidence that it would not. And Russian action in setting up Communist regimes in the Balkans indicated that they had no intention of giving the people involved a choice. Both documents referred to the Atlantic Charter, but when the Declaration on Liberated Europe was under discussion Churchill said that he would agree to it "as long as it was clearly understood that the reference to the Atlantic Charter did not apply to the British Empire."

There was a similar discrepancy between the President's statement when he returned from Yalta and the facts of the conference. F.D.R. said:

The Crimean Conference was a successful effort by the three leading nations to find a common ground for peace. It spells the end of the system of unilateral action and exclusive alliances and spheres of influence and balances of power and all the other expedients which have been tried for centuries—and have failed. We propose to substitute for all these a universal organization in which all peace-loving nations will finally have a chance to join.

The decisions on Poland and the Far East were clearly based on Russia's concern for its sphere of influence.

In the light of the supposed necessity of Russian military cooperation in Europe and the Pacific area, Ambassador Harriman's clear statement of Russian political purpose was ignored. Just before the Yalta Conference he had written:

> The overriding consideration in Soviet foreign policy is the preoccupation with "security" as Moscow sees it. This objective explains most of the recent Soviet actions which have roused criticism abroad. . . . The Soviet conception of "security" does not appear cognizant of the similar needs or rights of other countries and of Russia's obligation to accept the restraints as well as the benefits of an international security system.

Churchill was somewhat more restrained than Roosevelt as to the results of the Yalta Conference. He told the House of Commons, "Hope has been powerfully strengthened by our meeting in the Crimea," but he added, "We are now entering a world of imponderables, and at every stage occasions for self-questioning arise. It is a mistake to look too far ahead. Only one link in the chain of destiny can be handled at a time."

Public reaction to what was announced on the results at Yalta was not quite so enthusiastic as on previous occasions. This was principally because of the Polish settlement, which Polish-Americans loudly labeled as "The Rape of Poland." There was also some criticism of the voting procedure settlement along the lines that Roosevelt had "sold out" to the Russians. This is hard to understand, since the settlement was based on Soviet acceptance of the United States' proposal. The Far Eastern deal and the agreement on membership for two Soviet republics were kept secret.

The principal complainants outside the United States were the Latin American republics. Their reaction to being ignored in the planning for a postwar United Nations had progressed from displeasure to very vocal anger after Dumbarton Oaks. Prior to the spring of 1945 the United States paid little attention to the opinions of its southern neighbors and gave scant heed to keeping them informed on what was going on in planning an organization in which they would represent 40 percent of the initial members. In 1939, at a Pan-American meeting in Panama, a committee had been appointed which had the specific responsibility of formulating inter-American proposals for a world organization. This committee was completely ignored. This disregard for the small states also applied to the smaller powers of Europe.

It is true that the Russians probably would not have participated in conversations which included any of the smaller states. Their thinking on a postwar organization was in terms of a three power—or, reluctantly, a four or five power—alliance. But in the minds of most critics this does not excuse the State Department for not having given the Latin American states an opportunity to express their ideas before Dumbarton Oaks.

After the Dumbarton Oaks Conversations the State Department tried to mend its fences by holding a series of meetings with Latin American representatives in Blair House. These, perhaps, made things worse. The State Department took the attitude that they were educational rather than consultative. They told their southern neighbors what was going on, in rather vague terms. The purpose of the meetings, they said, was to arrive at "a common informed understanding" in support of the Dumbarton Oaks Proposals—but the Proposals were not available for discussion throughout most of the meetings. The upshot of this was a strong Latin American demand for a full and formal Pan-American meeting. This was held in Mexico City immediately after Yalta.

By this time—the end of February, 1945—the six "associated" Latin American republics had declared war on the Axis and were now eligible for membership in the United Nations. Only Argentina, which had a pro-Nazi government, was out in the cold and was not allowed to participate at Mexico City. As a result of sanctions against it proposed there, Argentina declared war late in March.

As soon as the Mexico City Conference opened, the Latin American states started to demand changes in the Dumbarton Oaks Proposals. There were seven areas of change in which the other states were generally agreed. They wanted to establish a goal of universal membership; to amplify the purposes and principles of the organization; to do the same for the General Assembly; to extend the jurisdiction of the International Court; to create an agency to promote "intellectual and moral cooperation" among nations; to assure the solution of inter-American controversies and questions by inter-American methods and procedures; and to secure adequate representation for Latin America on the Security Council.

It soon became evident that what the southern states really wanted was to strengthen and expand Pan-Americanism to form a sort of United Nations of the Western Hemisphere. They were far more interested in their regional organization than in the world organization. They were willing to agree that the regional organization should conform to the purposes of the world organization and that on certain matters the Security Council should have supervisory jurisdiction. But they wanted this authority to be defined within the narrowest possible limits. In short, they wanted to settle Western Hemisphere problems within the Western Hemisphere.

This was excellent proof of how far the Good Neighbor policy had progressed in twelve years. Back in 1919, one important reason why the U.S. Senate would not endorse the Covenant of the League of Nations was that it did not make adequate provision for the regional agreement represented by the Monroe Doctrine. At that time the Latin American states joined the League, claiming that there was no regional agreement in the Western Hemisphere. The United States had never asked them to agree to anything; it had merely applied the Monroe Doctrine as it saw fit. Now the principle of the Monroe Doctrine had become multilateral, and it was the states south of the border which were insisting that it must not be violated by a world organization.

The Pan-American states had previously agreed on mutual resistance to foreign aggression. Now they wanted to establish machinery for enforcement to settle internal Western Hemisphere disputes. They wanted to expand the inter-American machinery concerned with educational and cultural affairs. They wanted to do all this fast, so that the expanded regional organization would be a *fait accompli* before the San Francisco Conference. And they wanted to have a Charter. In passing, all of this led to the creation of the Organization of American States in 1948 —which does have a Charter similar to that of the United Nations.

To the United States delegates at Mexico City the demands of the Latin American states broke dangerous ground. If they agreed to a largely autonomous regional organization in the Western Hemisphere—particularly as to security—how could they oppose similar autonomous regional organizations established by Russia in Eastern Europe or by Great Britain in what it considered its sphere of influence? Also, they could not go to San Francisco with the Dumbarton Oaks Proposals in one hand and a conflicting set of resolutions adopted at Mexico City in the other.

The matter was finally settled by a masterful use of "weasel" words in the Mexico City Resolutions. This document expressed the feelings, desires, and opinions of the Latin American states, but the United States delegates inserted qualifying clauses so that it could be interpreted as conforming to the Dumbarton Oaks Proposals. An example is the following paragraph in which the changes made by the United States are indicated in italics:

The above Declaration and Recommendation constitute a regional arrangement for dealing with such matters relating to the maintenance of international peace and security *as are appropriate for regional action in this Hemisphere.* The said arrangement . . . *shall be consistent with the purposes and principles of the general international organization,* when established.

The United States delegation to the San Francisco Conference had been picked at Yalta. Secretary of State Stettinius wanted to defer to ex-Secretary Hull as chairman of the delegation because of the dominant role that the latter had played in the formative period. Hull was too ill to attend and Stettinius led the group. Unlike Woodrow Wilson's all-Democrat group, with no representation from Congress, which went to Paris to create the League, the San Francisco delegation would be truly bipartisan with ample congressional representation. The senior members of both parties on the Senate Foreign Relations Committee and the House Foreign Affairs Committee were included, as was Harold Stassen, former Republican governor of Minnesota. Republican John Foster Dulles was senior Republican adviser. Even sex was considered by the inclusion of Dean Virginia Gildersleeve of Barnard College. Franklin Delano Roosevelt, the man who had started the whole thing, died thirteen days before the San Francisco Conference opened.

The emotional enthusiasm and hope for the United Nations are indicated by this description of the scene in the Senate as the delegation prepared to leave for the Golden Gate:

As the Senator [Vandenberg] ended his remarks there was a sudden stirring of emotions such as the staid old Chamber had seldom witnessed. On both sides of the aisle men were getting to their feet, clapping their hands in violation of the Senate rules, and, after a moment, surging across the Chamber to shake hands, to put their arms around the shoulders of the two delegates and wish them well. America was going to San Francisco—to the second great international effort to establish lasting peace in the world—in a manner far removed from the lonely pilgrimage of Woodrow Wilson to Paris hardly a generation before.

7

Conflict and Compromise

The city by the Golden Gate was crowded in late April, 1945, as the participants gathered for the United Nations Conference on International Organization. There were only 282 delegates from fifty nations, but their staffs swelled this total to 1,726 persons. They were aided by an International Secretariat numbering 1,058 and served by 2,263 military personnel, 400 members of the Red Cross, 800 members of the American Women's Volunteer Services, and 800 Boy Scouts; plus 188 telephone and telegraph operators. Hovering over all these—or getting underfoot— were 2,636 members of the international press and radio services. A few unofficial hangers-on undoubtedly swelled the total of those who were in some way involved in drafting the Charter of the United Nations to well over 10,000.

During the two months of the conference the average

daily output of documents used about half a million sheets of paper; in all, seventy-eight tons of paper were used, not including the production of the press representatives. Dean Gildersleeve, fresh from her ivory tower, found the "blinding blaze of publicity" in which the conference was held to be "rather disconcerting."

Although hope and enthusiasm were the prevailing moods for most of the participants, Russia immediately made it apparent that all was not going to be sweetness and light. It had been agreed at Yalta that the United States and Great Britain would support the Russian request, to be made to the conference, that the two Soviet republics be admitted to the United Nations. Now, delegations from the Ukraine and White Russia showed up and the Soviets insisted that they be seated without further question. Also, they demanded that a delegation from the Lublin government of Poland be seated, although they had done nothing to establish the broader provisional government that they had promised.

The Anglo-Americans took a firm stand on Poland, and its delegation was not admitted. The Latin American states strenuously opposed the admission of the Russian republics but were voted down. However, Russia was over-ruled in its opposition to seating Argentina, which had declared war on the Axis only a few days previously. Denmark was admitted before the conference ended. The final list of participants included:

Argentina	Byelorussia (White Russia)
Australia	Soviet Socialist Republic
Belgium	Canada
Bolivia	Chile
Brazil	China

Colombia

Costa Rica

Czechoslovakia

Denmark

Dominican Republic

Ecuador

Egypt

El Salvador

Ethiopia

France

Greece

Guatemala

Haiti

Honduras

India

Iran

Iraq

Lebanon

Liberia

Luxembourg

Mexico

Netherlands

New Zealand

Nicaragua

Norway

Panama

Paraguay

Peru

Philippine Commonwealth

Saudi Arabia

Syria

Turkey

Ukrainian Soviet Socialist Republic

Union of South Africa

Union of Soviet Socialist Republics

United Kingdom

United States

Uruguay

Venezuela

Yugoslavia

An analysis of this list indicates that Russia had good cause to fear that it might be swamped by an Anglo-American coalition, particularly when it is remembered that the Russians believed that the Latin American states and the British Dominions were controlled by their big brothers in the same manner as Russian satellites. This would give the United States twenty-one votes from the Western Hemisphere plus sure support from the Philippines and Liberia, two votes short of a majority. Great Britain would have six votes with her Dominions and India plus almost sure support from Greece, Lebanon, Turkey, and five Arab states. Russia could count on no outside support except, perhaps, from the two Slavic countries.

Actually, among the Big Three, Russia was in the strongest bargaining position at San Francisco because it had the least interest in forming a general international organization. If the conference failed an alternative might be simply a Big Power alliance. This would have satisfied Russia, which had no interest in small states that it did or might not dominate. As another alternative, the United States might have pulled out of a European alliance; and nothing could have pleased Russia better than for the United States to retreat to isolationism.

Throughout his stay at the conference Soviet Foreign Minister Molotov was rudely impatient with the concern that was shown for the opinions of the small states. At the first meeting of the Steering Committee he insulted Mexico's Foreign Minister by inferring that his remarks were dictated by the United States. This infuriated all the Latin American representatives, but their main concern—and the concern of the other small states—was less with Russia than with the predominant role which the Dumbarton Oaks Proposals gave to the major powers as a group. The primary problem of the San Francisco Conference was to bring about agreement between the small states and the big ones, to keep as much of the Dumbarton Oaks Proposals as possible and still make them palatable to the minor nations. Although their interests were not identical, the Latin American countries and the Arab states—with only one tenth of the world's population—represented half the votes at the conference. They could not be ignored.

Another purpose of the conference was to put the Dumbarton Oaks Proposals into properly impressive language. As one British commentator wrote: "The Dumbarton Oaks Proposals have been criticized as lacking in humanity and warmth. They were indeed drafted by officials who were anxious to avoid using language which, by emotional appeal, would obscure the actual facts of the international situation. It is no doubt advisable to include in such a document aspirations which the authors know cannot be immediately realized, to make, as it were, an appeal to posterity. But that is a process better left to politicians, and they eventually did all that was necessary in this respect at San Francisco."

The conference was organized with an Executive Committee of fourteen states, a Steering Committee of one representative from each state, and twelve technical committees within which were numerous commissions. These groups went over the Dumbarton Oaks Proposals line by line and considered in the same way nearly 1,200 amendments that were proposed. After these had been consolidated or redrafted, those that were still under consideration were reported out to the conference, where a two-thirds vote was necessary for passage.

While the general conference was in progress the Big Five held a separate conference. The United States, Great Britain, the U.S.S.R., China, and France were called the Sponsoring Powers of the general conference, although in fact France had refused to join with the other four in inviting the remaining United Nations to the meeting. Charles de Gaulle's prominent nose was out of joint because he had not been invited to Yalta. Most of the amendments to the Dumbarton Oaks Proposals that were finally adopted at San Francisco came out of these Big Power meetings. However, in the main, these represented revisions of demands that had been made by smaller states.

In the final Charter there were suprisingly few important deviations from the Dumbarton Oaks Proposals. Most of the changes were in language, to spell out more clearly certain aspects of the Proposals and to make them more acceptable to the small states. The latter were primarily concerned about the extensive powers of the Security Council in relation to the General Assembly; the veto power as it applied to disputes in which no permanent member was a party; the restrictions on the operation of regional organizations; and the provision that amendments to the Charter had to be unanimously ratified by the Big Five, who also had exclusive power to propose new members. The small states also had much to say about justice, human rights, and fundamental freedoms, although the fervor of many of these speeches often seemed to be in reverse ratio to the practice of those who were making them.

In one respect the small states had lost ground under the proposed Charter in relation to their position under the League Covenant. In the League Council no action could be taken except by unanimous agreement; every state, large and small, had a veto power. Because this had never worked, the small states were willing to accept the basic security system outlined in the Dumbarton Oaks Proposals, and its main structure was passed with little debate. But there were many and diverse attempts to weaken the role of the major powers on the Security Council, few of which succeeded.

Among the amendments that did not pass were some designed to break down the basic differentiation between the Security Council and the General Assembly; to increase the size of the Council by adding three or four more small states; and to limit the rights of permanent members to veto pacific-settlement decisions in disputes in which they were not a party. Among the amendments that did get passed was one that provided that parties to a dispute who were not members of the Council could sit as members during the consideration of their disputes. It was also agreed that states from whom contingents of armed forces were required for an enforcement action would be permitted "to participate in the decisions of the Security Council concerning the employment of contingents of that member's armed forces." This, in effect, would at times increase the representation of the small states.

The small states tried to limit the authority and the veto power of the Security Council, in practice, by having many things spelled out in detail. For instance, the Proposals stated what the Council might do should a state become an aggressor, but did not define an aggressor. Bolivia proposed to change this by adding this description of an aggressor:

A state shall be designated an aggressor if it has committed any of the following acts to the detriment of another state:
(a) Invasion of another state's territory by armed forces.
(b) Declaration of war.
(c) Attack by land, sea, or air forces, with or without declaration of war, on another state's territory, shipping, or aircraft.
(d) Support given to armed bands for the purpose of invasion.
(e) Intervention in another state's internal or foreign affairs.
(f) Refusal to submit the matter which has caused a dispute to the peaceful means provided for its settlement.
(g) Refusal to comply with a judicial decision lawfully pronounced by an international court.

It was proposed that sanctions against a state which performed any one of these listed acts should be automatic and consequently not subject to a veto. The large states opposed this on the grounds that no prior list of what constituted acts of aggression could be all-inclusive in every situation, and acts that were defined as aggression might, under certain circumstances, be construed as acts of self-defense. Czechoslovakia pointed out that when it was threatened by Germany in 1939, France and England had deterred it from taking defensive measures on the ground that such action might be labeled by Germany as aggression. After much debate the language of the Proposals was retained; the Security Council was left with "the entire decision as to what constitutes a threat to peace, a breach of the peace, or an act of aggression."

In passing it might be remarked that, had the Bolivian amendment been accepted, the United Nations would have been required to automatically apply sanctions against the United States as an aggressor at the time of the Bay of Pigs invasion of Cuba. The help which the United States supplied to this action clearly violated section (d) of the Bolivian definition of an aggressor.

Considering the importance President Roosevelt had attached to disarmament in his early thinking of a new international order, it is surprising that there was virtually no discussion on this subject at San Francisco. The reason may have been psychological—in the midst of a war the immediate concern was to produce armaments, not to limit them. The Charter followed the Proposals in giving the General Assembly authority to "consider the general principles of cooperation in the maintenance of international peace and security, including the principles govern-

ing disarmament and the regulation of armaments." The
Security Council could formulate plans and submit them
to members for establishing a system that would "promote
the establishment of international peace and security with
the least diversion of the world's human and economic resources." In short, the United Nations could study and advise its members on arms limitation but had no enforcement authority.

At the time these decisions were made the existence of
an atomic bomb was unknown to any of the delegates. On
the very day that the conference opened, Secretary of War
Stimson informed President Truman of the anticipated
success of the new weapon and said:

The world in its present state of moral advancement com-
pared with its technical development would be eventually at
the mercy of such a weapon. In other words, modern civilization might be completely destroyed.

To approach any world peace organization of any pattern
now likely to be considered, without an appreciation by the
leaders of our country of the power of this new weapon, would
seem to be unrealistic. No system of control heretofore considered would be adequate to control this menace. Both inside
any particular country and between the nations of the world,
the control of this weapon will undoubtedly be a matter of the
greatest difficulty and would involve such thorough-going
rights of inspection and internal controls as we have never
heretofore contemplated.

It has been said that the Charter of the United Nations
is "preatomic" and that, had the existence of the bomb
been known, there would have been a demand at San
Francisco for some stronger and more positive means of
controlling atomic weapons. Had the bomb been exploded
before the conference it would surely have led to further

discussion of control, but it is certain that the United States, which then had exclusive possession of this formidable weapon, would have refused to give up its "domestic jurisdiction" and place the bomb under international control.

The most extensive debate at San Francisco ranged around the subject of the veto power by a permanent member of the Security Council. The Yalta formula provided that a major power could veto any "substantive" matter before the Council, unless it was a party to a dispute, in which case it must abstain from voting. But the formula did not define when a matter ceased to be "procedural" and became "substantive"—and there was much else that it did not make clear to the small states. In fact, as the discussion developed, it turned out that the big states were not in agreement among themselves as to what the formula meant.

In general, the small states did not challenge the veto power in relation to enforcement action. They did question it in relation to all else. The New Zealand delegation set up the framework for subsequent debate with an opening query on how the veto would work. They said:

We want to know how far . . . can a matter in which a permanent Power is involved be taken before that Power can exercise its right to vote and veto any important matter on which it feels deeply? . . . How far can the Security Council go? Can it discuss matters freely and without limitation? Can it suggest proposals for settlement of a dispute? Can it inferentially throw upon the Power concerned the responsibility of refusing to accept and nullifying that decision of the Council? Can the Security Council designate one of its five permanent members as an aggressor, or can it simply point in that direction without such designation? . . .

Then in regard to a dispute in which one of the five permanent Powers is not immediately and directly involved: When
can one of the permanent Powers arbitrarily dissent from
and prevent any action? Can the matter be discussed in a
preliminary stage? Say there is a dispute involving danger of
war developing between two of the smaller Powers—can the
matter be brought up at the Security Council? When it is
brought up, how far can it be taken? Can it be fully discussed
right up to the point when number one decision . . . has to
be taken? . . . Can one Power prevent that matter being
made the subject of consideration by the Council?

These questions, and scores more like them, were referred to a special committee consisting of the Big Five and
a Little Five—Australia, Cuba, Egypt, the Netherlands,
and Greece. All questions were boiled down to a twenty-
three-point questionnaire which the Little Five presented
to the Big Five for explanation. Wading through the thou-
sands of pages of minutes and memoranda one gets the impression that there was more double talk than explanation.
The major powers were adamant that the Yalta formula be
preserved and the attitude of four of them was a very po-
lite "take it or leave it." The Soviets said the same thing,
but not politely. Senator Vandenberg commented on the
American position by noting in his diary:

This "veto" bizness is making it very difficult to maintain
any semblance of the fiction of "sovereign equality" among
the nations. . . . It is fully justified in respect to the use of
force because the Powers with a "veto" will be the Powers
which must largely furnish the force. But it is immoral and
indefensible . . . in any other application. But the irony of
the situation is that the greater the extent of the "veto" the
more impossible it becomes for the new League to involve
America in *anything* against our own will. Therefore, the
greater the "veto" the easier it becomes to fight off our critics

in Congress, in the country and in the press when the new Treaty faces its ratification battle. (Every cloud has a silver lining.)

The Soviet interpretation of the Yalta formula was that a permanent member could veto almost anything except a dispute to which it was a party, including the right of the Council to even discuss a matter. The rest of the major powers held that a decision to discuss a given matter was essentially procedural and therefore could be made by the affirmative vote of any seven members. The Soviets claimed that this was a substantive matter, subject to veto. Their memorandum on this subject ended with the statement: "a discussion on a dispute is of great political importance by itself and may entail serious consequences; therefore, the question, whether a dispute should be considered, in no way can be deemed a procedural matter."

Senator Vandenberg graphically described the impasse resulting from the Soviet position by writing in his diary:

The *big* crisis broke last night. Gromyko was ready with his answer from Moscow to the main question bedeviling the Conference—namely, shall the Big Five be able to "veto" even a *discussion* or *consideration* of a question brought to the Security Council? We have been waiting ten days for this. The answer—Russia demands her "veto" even on *free speech* in the Council. This collides with the grim conviction of almost every other Power at Frisco. It is "Yalta" carried to the final, absurd extreme. When Gromyko made his report to us in the Pent-House, we all know that we had reached the "zero hour" of this great adventure. With what seemed to be finality, the Soviet said they could not accept our proposal of "free discussion." We all knew that none of the rest of us can accept the Soviet view. Did it mean the immediate breakup of the Conference? Did it mean going on to a Charter without Russia? Instead of precipitating a showdown, Secretary Stettinius adjourned the meeting until this morning. Meanwhile he phoned Truman and Hull both of whom said we must irrevocably reject the Soviet position.

At this juncture President Truman instructed Ambassador Harriman and Harry Hopkins (who was in Moscow) to see Stalin personally:

. . . and ask him whether he realizes fully what the instructions sent to Gromyko mean and what effect the Soviet proposal would have upon the character of the world organization we are all trying to work out. Please tell him in no uncertain words that this country could not possibly join an organization based on so unreasonable an interpretation of the provision of the great powers in the Security Council.

After hearing the Americans, Stalin grudgingly said that the matter was of little significance and that he would accede to the American position.

This inner squabble among the Big Five had to do with *extending* the veto power in the Yalta formula. Stalin's agreement did not in any way liberalize this formula, and the small states continued to press for this, but to no avail. When Australia and Canada proposed exempting certain decisions from the veto, Senator Tom Connally replied that the permanent members would go no further. He recorded that he said: "You can go home from San Francisco —if you wish, I cautioned the delegates, and report that you have defeated the veto. . . . But you can also say, 'We *tore up the Charter.*' At this point I sweepingly ripped the Charter draft in my hands to shreds and flung the scraps upon the table."

The other subject of extensive debate at San Francisco dealt with regional agreements. The small states were to some extent successful in securing greater autonomy for regional organizations than was provided in the Dumbarton Oaks Proposals. This whole subject was complicated by a difference of interests among various groups. The Latin Americans wanted to protect the Western Hemisphere organization, particularly the right to take autonomous action against aggression in this area, from within or without, that had been agreed on in the Act of Chapultepec-adopted at Mexico City. The Australians and New Zealanders, and the Arab states, wanted to establish the basis for new, largely autonomous organizations in their parts of the world. It had already been agreed that security against new aggression on the part of the Axis countries would be, at least temporarily, outside the scope of the new world organization. To this end Russia had already made mutual assistance pacts with France and Czechoslovakia. There was a demand that such treaties should be considered as regional agreements under which action could be taken without recourse to the Security Council.

All of these conflicting aims brought a flood of proposed amendments from several directions. Referring to the mutual assistance treaties, Vandenberg summarized the American position by writing:

Europe would have freedom of action for her defensive regional arrangements . . . but the Western Hemisphere would *not* have similar freedom of action under its Pan-American agreements. . . . Therefore, in the event of trouble in the Americas, we could not act ourselves; we would have to depend exclusively on the Security Council; and any one permanent member of the Council could veto the latter action (putting us at the mercy of Britain, Russia or China). Thus little is left of the Monroe Doctrine.

The Dumbarton Oaks Proposals had provided: "Nothing in the Charter should preclude the existence of regional arrangements or agencies." But they had further provided that "no enforcement action should be taken under regional arrangements or by regional agencies without the authorization of the Security Council."

This subordination of their regional organization was galling to the Latin American states. The problem was finally solved by an application of the principle of self-defense. This is so obviously an inalienable right of any sovereign state that it had not previously been discussed. Now it was injected and broadened to include collective as well as individual self-defense. It is reasonable to assume that any breach of the peace involving one state in the Western Hemisphere might call for action in the name of self-defense by other states. This was embraced in a new article in the Charter, number fifty-one, which read:

Nothing in the present Charter shall impair the inherent right of individual or collective self-defense if an armed attack occurs against a Member of the United Nations, until the Security Council has taken the measures necessary to maintain international peace and security. Measures taken by Members in the exercise of this right of self-defense shall be immediately reported to the Security Council and shall not in any way affect the authority and responsibility of the Security Council under the present Charter to take at any time such action as it deems necessary in order to maintain or restore international peace and security.

This article is probably the most significant single difference between the Dumbarton Oaks Proposals and the Charter of the United Nations. When it was adopted, said Vandenberg, "the Latin cheers took the roof off."

Discussions of the authority and powers of the General Assembly ended with more or less hair-splitting distinctions in wording. In general, the small states sought to strengthen the General Assembly at the expense of the Security Council. Some of their amendments sought to associate the Assembly with the Council in enforcement decisions. They also wanted the Charter so worded that there would be no question of the right of the Assembly to act as a "town meeting of the world" without restrictions as to what subjects it could discuss and what courses of action it could recommend.

The Dumbarton Oaks Proposals provided that the General Assembly should receive reports from the Security Council, and an effort was made to give the Assembly the right to approve or disapprove these reports. This was killed on the grounds that if the Assembly disapproved an action of the Council it would leave the two organs acting at cross purposes, with no supreme authority. In matters of security the authority was in the Council, under the Dumbarton Oaks Proposals, and there it remained.

No basic change was made in the role of the Assembly at San Francisco, but its authority was spelled out in more detail. It might be said that its position in having a moral influence on events was somewhat enhanced It was readily agreed that each member state could have five representatives in the Assembly but only one vote. Decisions on routine matters would be by a simple majority; on important questions a two-thirds majority was required. There was some debate on the method of electing new members and of selecting the Secretary General, but here the difference had to do with the pre-eminent role played by the Security Council in these matters.

Most of the Latin American delegates wanted to make membership open to "all sovereign states that now exist or which in the future may exist under their own independent conditions of life," as Brazil put it. But even the most ardent advocate of universal membership admitted that the enemy states could not be admitted until they had shown conclusive evidence of reform. The phrase "peace-loving" was finally retained from the Dumbarton Oaks Proposals, and the resulting clause read: "Membership of the Organization is open to all peace-loving states which, in the judgment of the Organization, are able and ready to accept and carry out the obligations contained in the Charter." The small states put up a strenuous fight to give the General Assembly complete authority on the admission of new members, but lost to the original Dumbarton Oaks system, under which new members must be recommended by the Security Council.

The small states also lost their fight to have the election of the Secretary General independent of the Security Council, but a Soviet proposal that there be four Deputy Secretary Generals was defeated. The original Soviet idea was that these five would be from the major powers, with the top job rotating. The Russians first backed down to the extent of saying that they did not care where four of them came from so long as the fifth was a Russian. The whole idea of deputies was defeated, but the principle that the Secretary General be recommended by the Security Council was retained.

The small states had high hopes for the Economic and Social Council and easily secured support for making it one of the principal organs of the United Nations. Dumbarton Oaks had specified only the Council, Assembly,

Court, and Secretariat in this category. As with other organs, the small states sought to enlarge the Economic and Social Council, so that they would have more opportunity for representation on it. They did not succeed in this. There were some amendments that proposed rather fantastic objectives for this organ, but in the main the changes that were accepted merely spelled out the Dumbarton Oaks Proposals in more detail.

Dumbarton Oaks had merely said that the international organization should "facilitate solutions of international economic, social and other humanitarian problems and promote respect for human rights and fundamental freedoms." Now, specific reference was added to health, cultural, and educational concerns, and it was made plain that the respect for human rights and fundamental freedoms was for all, "without distinction as to race, language, religion or sex."

The extent to which wording was scrutinized in every line of the Charter is evidenced by the attitude of the United States toward a reference to education. It was proposed that the United Nations should promote solutions of international economic, social, health, educational, and cultural problems. The United States delegation objected to this on the grounds that education was a domestic matter. It was finally decided that "solutions" should be sought for the other problems but only "cooperation" should be expected in connection with educational and cultural affairs.

The United States delegates also objected to the use of the words "full employment" in a description of the objectives of the Economic and Social Council. This, they said, was also a matter of internal concern, and the Senate would not ratify a document which might bind the country to international participation in some form of collectivism. Because of the separate clause in the Charter which prohibited the organization from interfering in the internal affairs of any member, the United States finally backed down on this.

Among the other proposals to expand the scope of the Economic and Social Council were some dealing with immigration, raw materials, and postwar reconstruction. The last was already being handled by a specialized agency; the first was clearly an internal matter. Although "access, on equal terms to the trade and to the raw materials of the world" had been specifically mentioned in the Atlantic Charter, any such reference was voted down in the Charter of the United Nations. It was felt that the full scope of international economic problems included many other things than trade and raw materials and that mention of any particular aspects might tend to limit the area of interest of the Economic and Social Council.

The San Francisco Conference was handicapped in considering the subject of colonialism and trusteeship because these subjects were not covered in the Dumbarton Oaks Proposals. The only working papers available were the dissimilar proposals of the United States State Department and the British Foreign Office. These were used, together with amendments of others of the Big Five, as a working paper for the committee of the general conference, which was responsible for these matters. However, since the Big Five did not agree among themselves, progress was difficult and was further complicated by the necessity for the Soviet delegates to refer everything to Moscow for decision. This was regular Russian practice, but it was more complicating in this area because there had been no basic decision, other than the vague statement in the Yalta declaration.

It was evident that Great Britain and France had no intention of permitting the United Nations to have any authority to interfere with their colonial systems. Great Britain still bridled at the word "independence," which China and the Soviet Union wanted to use in connection with a statement on the objective of developing self-government. France, too, favored the idea of self-government in the form of some kind of federal unity with the mother country. The French felt that the proposed language would encourage the "hatching" of many small, independent states which were not ready for total self-government—as, in fact, it did.

The final Charter contained three chapters on nonself-governing territories and trusteeship, in which the French and British view prevailed. In connection with colonies, the members of the United Nations proclaimed a moral obligation to "develop self-government, to take due account of the political aspirations of the peoples, and to assist them in the progressive development of their free political institutions, according to the particular circumstances of each territory and its peoples and their varying stages of advancement." They also agreed to submit information to the Secretary General "relating to economical, social and educational conditions" in colonies; but this was subject to "such limitations as security and constitutional considerations may require."

The Charter established an International Trusteeship System and a Trusteeship Council, but these applied only to previously mandated territories, those detached from enemy states, and those "voluntarily placed under the system by states responsible for their administration." In any trusteeship agreement part or all of the territory might be designated as a strategic area, and all functions of the United Nations relating to such areas "shall be exercised by the Security Council."

The Charter also provided that "nothing in this Charter shall be construed in or of itself to alter in any manner the rights whatsoever of any states or any peoples or the terms of existing international instruments to which Members of the United Nations may respectively be parties." In short, despite Roosevelt's strong feelings on imperialism and the use of trusteeship to lead dependent peoples to independence, the United Nations would have no authority to interfere with prewar colonialism or even to advise on or supervise questions of self-determination except under the limited trusteeship system.

Before the San Francisco Conference a commission of international jurists had met and prepared a Statute for the International Court of Justice. They had left a few things blank which had political overtones. These were to be decided at San Francisco. One such subject was whether the Court was to be a new organ of the United Nations or a continuation of the old Court that had been associated with the League of Nations. Since the statute that they proposed was a revision of the statute of the old Court with merely minor changes, this would seem to be a distinction without a difference. However, there was both a legal and a psychological point involved. The Statute of the Court would become part of the Charter of the United Nations. But some members of the old Court were not members of the United Nations and, as enemy states, were not eligible for membership. And some members of the

United Nations, including the United States, were not members of the old Court. If the old Court were retained, the United States could not ratify the Charter without becoming a member of it, something which the Senate repeatedly had refused to do for over twenty-five years. From a practical standpoint it was therefore decided to label the judicial body as "new," although in practice it was a continuation of the existing Court.

The big question in connection with the Court had to do with compulsory jurisdiction. The commission of the jurists had presented alternate proposals. Under one, all members of the United Nations recognized the jurisdiction of the Court, on certain questions, as compulsory. Under the other, members "may" recognize the Court's jurisdiction as compulsory—but, on the other hand, they might not. The legal matters involved were any question of international law; interpretation of treaties; establishment of a fact which would constitute a breach of an international obligation; and determination of reparations for such a breach.

Everybody except the United States and the Soviet Union wanted the Court to have compulsory jurisdiction. The United States delegates said frankly that the Senate would not ratify a Charter which gave an international court compulsory jurisdiction. This was an old sore point. Many isolationists had declaimed at length on the danger of a Court without an American judge deciding to take the Panama Canal away from the United States. The jurisdiction of the Court was not made compulsory unless members to a dispute so desired.

The United States and the Soviet Union also opposed numerous proposals to give the Security Council power to enforce judgments of the Court if one party failed to abide by them. The United States pointed out that, if such failure resulted in a breach of the peace, the Security Council already had the necessary authority—subject to a permanent member veto. The matter was finally settled by a clause which provided that if a party failed to conform to a judgment of the Court the other party might appeal to the Security Council, "which may, if it deems necessary, make recommendations or decide upon measures to be taken to give effect to the judgment."

The first chapter of the Dumbarton Oaks Proposals had been labeled "Purposes"; the second "Principles." The Proposals contained no preamble, and there was no clear-cut distinction between purposes and principles; in fact, most of the principles listed in the Proposals were really obligations of members. There was much talk at San Francisco of trying to organize this material better, but the committee responsible reported that it "was very difficult, practically impossible, to draw a sharp and clear-cut distinction between what should be included under 'Purposes,' 'Principles,' or 'Preamble.' "

One important change was made in the list of general principles, having to do with the subject of domestic jurisdiction. In the Dumbarton Oaks Proposals this had been covered in the section on pacific settlements by a statement to the effect that the provision of this section "should not apply to situations or disputes arising out of matters which by international law are solely within the domestic jurisdiction of the state concerned." It was felt that this was in the wrong place—that it should be an underlying principle of the entire Charter. Also, there was no reference to non-intervention anywhere in the Charter, and this might be incorporated with domestic jurisdiction. Finally, before San Francisco, the United States had second thoughts on the words "international law" and wanted them out. It claimed that "the body of international law on this subject is indefinite and inadequate."

Several proposed amendments would have the question of whether or not a given matter was domestic decided by the International Court of Justice or by the General Assembly. The United States did not like this, either. In principle, the United States wanted to decide for itself what was domestic. The matter was finally settled by adding a seventh "principle" which said:

Nothing contained in the present Charter shall authorize the United Nations to intervene in matters which are essentially within the domestic jurisdiction of any state or shall require the Members to submit such matters to settlement under the present Charter; but this principle shall not prejudice the application of enforcement measures.

Before the San Francisco Conference, Field Marshal Jan Smuts of the Union of South Africa had addressed a meeting of the British Commonwealth countries to urge that the Charter be introduced by a preamble setting forth, "in language which should appeal to the heart as well as the mind of men, the purposes which the United Nations were setting themselves to achieve" and the "nobility of intention" of the founders. Smuts prepared a draft preamble and presented it at San Francisco where one commentator said that he was "a glamorous figure as he stood before the committee, still slender and straight in spite of his age, in his marshal's uniform with its decorations." Moved by the grand old man, the committee agreed by acclamation to accept the Smuts preamble—in principle. Then they went to work on it.

At first the United States delegation did not seem to have much interest in a preamble, although Harold Stassen said that it should be "short, moving and beautiful, something that every school child could commit to memory and that could hang, framed, in every cottage on the globe." Then Representative Sol Bloom said that he was ready to "insist upon and, if necessary, fight for the preamble to begin with: 'We, the People.' " Whereupon Dean Gildersleeve, professor of literature and American member of the committee, redrafted Smuts' version to begin. "We, THE PEOPLE OF THE UNITED NATIONS determined to save succeeding generations from the scourge of war, which in our time has brought untold sorrow to mankind . . ."

There were other suggestions from Belgium and Columbia, and all of these were wrangled over. Dean Gildersleeve recorded: "The delegates of the various nations fell to arguing strenuously from the philosophical point of view, from the literary point of view, from the political point of view." What finally emerged is not something that every school child will commit to memory. It is virtually impossible to develop good literary style in a committee. The resultant preamble is not very good prose; is not, in fact, very good grammar. It starts with the words "We, the People" despite the fact that this phrase translates very awkwardly in the languages of many member nations. Also, the *people* of most countries had no legal right to adopt a Charter—this was a function of government. The legal eagles at San Francisco got around this—and completely ruined any style that the preamble might have had —by tacking onto its end the statement:

Accordingly, our respective governments, through representatives assembled in the city of San Francisco, who have exhibited their full powers found to be in good and due form, have
agreed to the present Charter of the United Nations and do
hereby establish an international organization to be known as
the United Nations.

In the final days of the San Francisco Conference some
of the delegates became impatient. The war in Europe had
ended. There was to be a top-level conference at Potsdam
in July on many important immediate aspects of the peace.
There was a desire to have the Charter completed before
the Potsdam meeting, and the United States wanted it in
time for ratification by the Senate before the adjournment
for the summer.

Some last-minute consideration was given to the interpretation of the Charter. There were proposals that it
should contain a clause covering this—some suggesting the
International Court and others the Assembly as the inter-
pretative organ. The big states were not in favor of this.
The committee reported:

It is to be understood, of course, that if an interpretation
made by any organ of the Organization or by a committee of
jurists is not generally acceptable it will be without binding
force. In such circumstances, or in cases where it is desired to
establish an authoritative interpretation as a precedent for the
future, it may be necessary to embody the interpretation in an
amendment to the Charter. This may always be accom-
plished by recourse to the procedure provided for amendment.

Amendments, of course, were subject to veto by the permanent members of the Security Council, so this meant
that, like so much else, the interpretation of the Charter
depended on big power unanimity.

Another last-minute consideration was a new look at the name of the organization. There was some argument that "United Nations" tied the organization too closely to the wartime alliance, and might militate against the concept of ultimate universal membership. In some languages the plural form of United Nations was difficult to translate. The Latin American delegates, in particular, wanted to consider such collective names as "community" or "association" in the title. After listening to much of this Dean Gildersleeve rose to express "the most earnest" hope that "our new world organization should be known as the United Nations, the name given to it by our great President," and the one under which "we can go forward to maintain the peace and to realize the dream of Franklin Roosevelt." The magic name of Roosevelt ended the debate.

It has been said that the last-minute rush at San Francisco prevented the refinement of the language of the Charter; that the prose could have been more efficacious if a final effort at polishing had been made. The Coordination Committee, which was responsible for this, might have been helped by more time; but this is not the main reason that many paragraphs of the Charter seem awkward or ambiguous. No amount of extra time would have permitted the committee to reword these paragraphs to everybody's satisfaction. Their awkwardness or ambiguity reflects an underlying difference of opinion as to their substance. If they were refined to more precise language these differences would have been highlighted—and the debates would have started over again. In short, some parts of the Charter are deliberately ambiguous, but it has good precedent for this—so are some parts of the Constitution of the

United States.

On June 25, 1945, exactly two months after the San Francisco Conference opened, the Charter was formally and unanimously adopted and presented in five official languages—Chinese, English, French, Russian, and Spanish. The last words in the otherwise staid minutes of the session were, "At this point, the delegates and the entire audience rose and cheered."

The Charter provided that the United Nations would come into being when ratifications were deposited with the United States government by the five permanent members of the Security Council plus a majority of the other signatories. The United States delegates at San Francisco had done their work well on anticipating every possible objection to the Charter on the part of the Senate. As a result of this, and because there was no question that public opinion was overwhelmingly favorable to a postwar United Nations, there was never a serious doubt that the Senate would consent to ratification.

When the Senate Committee on Foreign Relations held hearings on the Charter there were but few witnesses who opposed ratification; and some of these were "screwballs," like the one who considered the Charter a device of a British-Israel World Federation movement to set up a world state with the Duke of Windsor as king. Other opposition witnesses more or less canceled each other out. Those who feared that the United Nations would be a superstate in which the United States would lose its independence were balanced by those who opposed the organization because it was *not* a world state.

In its report to the Senate, the Foreign Relations Committee emphasized the freedom of action provided for the

United States by the Charter. They pointed out that specific commitments were either left to the future (such as military or arms regulation agreements) or surrounded by safeguards or reservations (as in the case of domestic and compulsory jurisdiction) or dependent on specific United States concurrence (as with the veto in the Security Council). The committee noted that "both the Monroe Doctrine and the inter-American system are effectively safeguarded under the Charter," and presented letters from the Secretaries of War and Navy stating that "the military and strategic implications" of the Charter were "in accord with the military interests of the United States."

Senate debate lasted for five days, primarily because numerous Senators wanted to speak "for the record." The only serious reservation proposed that might have led to trouble had to do with the right to commit American armed forces to action upon the vote of the United States representative on the Security Council without specific approval of Congress in each case. On this, Senator Vandenberg said:

> If we were to require the consent of Congress to every use of our armed forces, it would not only violate the spirit of the Charter, but it would violate the spirit of the Constitution of the United States, because under the Constitution the President has certain rights to use our armed forces in the national defense without consulting Congress. . . . It is just as much a part of the Constitution as is the congressional right to declare war. . . . I feel very deeply on the subject, because I totally sympathize with those who insist that in the final analysis the control of our entry into war shall remain in the Congress; on the other hand, I totally sympathize with the purpose of the Charter to use force to prevent situations where a declaration

of war is necessary. I think there is a sharp difference between the two.

It was further pointed out that this decision as to whether the executive or legislative branch of the government was to have certain authority was purely a domestic matter and therefore not a suitable subject for a reservation in ratifying the Charter. The matter could be decided when the special agreement with the Security Council on the use of armed forces, provided for in Article 43, came before the Senate. On this basis the Charter was ratified on July 28, 1945, by a vote of eighty-nine to two. Five Senators were absent, only one of whom would have voted against ratification. An unofficial tally is therefore ninety-three to three.

United States ratification had been preceded by Nicaragua and El Salvador. In their inimitable manner the Russians withheld ratification until theirs would be the deciding votes. After Egypt ratified as the twenty-fifth nation—including all of the other permanent members—the Soviets filed four ratifications in bulk: the U.S.S.R., the Ukraine, White Russia, and Poland. (By this time the Polish Provisional Government had been established and recognized.)

The Charter which fifty nations signed at San Francisco (and which is reproduced in full at the end of this chapter) contains 19 chapters divided into 111 articles. These, together with the 70 articles of the Statute of the International Court of Justice, represent a contract or treaty by which the signers voluntarily agree to cooperate in the promotion of certain common objectives. It is based on the principles of the sovereign equality of all member states, but recognizes that all states are not, in fact, equal. The five major powers that are permanent members of the Security Council are conceded greater authority and expected to take greater responsibility for the peace of the world.

The common objectives to which the signers agreed are spelled out in very broad terms in the four *Purposes of the United Nations:*

First, "To maintain international peace and security and, to that end, to take effective collective measures for the prevention and removal of threats to the peace. . . ." Second, "To develop friendly relations among nations based on respect for the principle of equal rights and self-determination of peoples. . . ." Third, "To achieve international cooperation in solving international problems of an economic, social, cultural, or humanitarian character, and in promoting and encouraging respect for human rights and for fundamental freedoms for all without distinction as to race, sex, language, or religion; and Fourth, "To be a center for harmonizing the actions of nations in the attainment of these common ends."

The first purpose aims at the achievement of one of Franklin Roosevelt's Four Freedoms—Freedom from Fear. The third purpose, with its reference to international economic problems and fundamental freedoms, embodies Roosevelt's other three freedoms—Freedom of Speech, Freedom of Religion, and Freedom from Want.

The balance of the Charter describes the physical character of the organization, on the one hand, and its functions and powers, on the other. Under the first classification it names and describes the principal organs—the General Assembly, the Security Council, the Economic and Social Council, the Trusteeship Council, the International Court of Justice, and the Secretariat. It prescribes the composition and procedures for each organ and deals with such general subjects as memberships, amendments, ratification.

Under the second classification the Charter spells out the purpose, powers, and functions of each organ. The General Assembly is covered in Chapter IV, the Security Council in Chapters V, VI, VII, and VIII. Chapter X covers the Economic and Social Council, but is preceded by a more definite statement of United Nations purposes in this area, in Chapter IX. This is likewise true of trusteeship. Chapter XIII covered the Trusteeship Council but is preceded by a *Declaration Regarding Nonself-governing Territories* in Chapter XI and an explanation of the International Trusteeship System in Chapter XII. The International Court of Justice is covered in Chapter XIV and the Secretariat in Chapter XV.

A very important article of the Charter is number twenty-two, which simply says: "The General Assembly may establish such subsidiary organs as it deems necessary for the performance of its functions." Actually, some of the specialized agencies which are associated with the United Nations under the supervision of the General Assembly were in existence before the general organization was completed. The International Labour Organization goes back to the end of World War I, and the Universal Postal Union was started in 1875. The United Nations Relief and Rehabilitation Administration started to function before the United Nations was organized and later became the International Refugee Organization, the functions of which were finally taken over by the United Nations High Commissioner for Refugees.

The new specialized agencies include the Food and Agriculture Organization (FAO), the International Civil Aviation Organization (ICAO), the United Nations Educational, Scientific, and Cultural Organization (UNESCO), the International Bank for Reconstruction and Development and its affiliate the International Finance Corporation (IFC), the International Monetary Fund, the Inter-Governmental Maritime Consultive Organization (IMCO), the International Telecommunication Union (ITU), the World Health Organization (WHO), and the World Meteorological Organization (WMO). For various reasons a few cooperating groups are not classified as specialized agencies, including the Commission on Narcotic Drugs, the International Atomic Energy Agency (IAEA) and the United Nations Children's Fund (UNICEF, because its original title was United Nations International Children's Emergency Fund.)

In their attitude toward the United Nations the people of the United States seem to be, like Caesar's Gaul, divided into three parts. First, there are those who consider it "the last, best, hope of the world." At the other end are those who label it "that bunch of atheists at the foot of Forty-second Street." Between these, and much larger, is that part of the populace which does not know much about it. Actually, many in the first and second groups are also members of the third.

It is not the function of this volume to evaluate the United Nations; if it can be of some help to that large middle group its purpose will be served. When the world organization first started to function there were high hopes that it would represent the final answer to world peace. Roosevelt had never expected this—nor did any other informed statesman. The Charter, and the world organization which it brought into being, were merely a first step. John Foster Dulles emphasized this in addressing the Senate committee at the time of ratification. He said:

I recognize that this Charter does not do what many people would like—to guarantee at a single step perpetual peace. . . . But the world does not move at a single step from a condition of virtual anarchy to a condition of well-rounded political order. Those steps are made falteringly. There are missteps; there have been missteps. This, for all I know, may again turn out to be a misstep. But . . . I say that here is, at least a step which presents itself to us, which may be, or which has a good chance to be, a step forward, onto new, firm, and higher ground. We cannot know that that is so, and [therefore], we must take precautions accordingly. But because we cannot know that it is so is certainly no reason to take no action at all. It may be that permanent peace will be achieved only by trial and error; but it will never be achieved at all if we are afraid even to try.

As soon as the United Nations started to function the Communists made it evident that they had no intention of cooperating with the other major powers to create the unanimity without which the organization could not hope to fully exercise its functions in the interests of world security. All of Roosevelt's hopes in this connection were in vain. The perfection of an atom bomb and intercontinental missiles by Russia soon brought about an armaments race against which the pre-World War II competition paled to insignificance. Despite Roosevelt's condemnation of spheres of influence and balance of power it was soon necessary for the United States to employ exactly this principle in fostering NATO in Europe and SEATO in the Pacific.

Yet, although the United Nations had not brought

about "freedom from fear," it undoubtedly has been effective in containing or preventing some situations which might have grown into more serious conflicts. Areas in which the United Nations has intervened include Iran, Albania, Greece, Cyprus, Palestine, Burma, Indonesia, Lebanon, Jordan, Egypt, the Congo, India-Pakistan, and principally Korea. None can say what might have been, but it is certainly reasonable to speculate that Russia might have taken more determined action to support North Korea and the Chinese Communists if the South Koreans had been supported only by the United States instead of the United Nations. Communists, like dictators, do not seem to care much for world opinion, but when that opinion is backed by machinery to apply world-wide sanctions and to organize world force, it may be counted on as a deterrent.

The United Nations is based on Roosevelt's ideals and ideas, but its Charter, of necessity, compromises with his principles, and thoughts. As one English historian said: "The statesman always seems to me in a non-moral position, because he has to consider what is possible as well as what is best, and the compromise is necessarily pitiable." The Charter of the United Nations is far from pitiable, but it does represent an effort to reconcile high principles with vested interests. Of course, most of the great institutions which are milestones in human progress were based on such compromises—including the Christian Church. The Magna Carta is highly idealistic, but it would be difficult to find a more selfish group of men than the barons who forced King John to accept it at Runnymede. Despite the fact that the world has not known freedom from fear during the first twenty years of the existence of the United Nations, there is reason to hope that it is fostering the slow spread of the high ideals on which it is based.

Perhaps Franklin Roosevelt best described the ultimate hope which the United Nations offers in a speech he made to the Foreign Missions Conference in 1940. The President said:

When the Apostles and Disciples of Christ crossed into Macedonia and visited one after another the countries of the Western world, they wrote a new chapter in human relations —for they carried for the first time a message of brotherhood, of faith and good-will and peace among men. . . .

The active search for peace which the early Christians preached meant meeting and overcoming those forces in the world which had set themselves against the brotherhood of man and which denied the equality of souls before the throne of God. In those olden days they faced apparently unconquerable forces—and yet were victorious. . . .

Today we seek a moral basis for peace. It cannot be a real peace if it fails to recognize brotherhood. It cannot be a lasting peace if the fruit of it is oppression, or starvation, or cruelty, or human life dominated by armed camps. It cannot be a sound peace if small nations must live in fear of powerful neighbors. It cannot be a moral peace if freedom from invasion is sold for tribute. It cannot be an intelligent peace if it denies free passage to that knowledge of those ideals which permit men to find common ground. It cannot be a righteous peace if worship of God is denied.

Appendix A:
Charter
of the United Nations

We the peoples of the United Nations determined

to save succeeding generations from the scourge of war, which twice in our lifetime has brought untold sorrow to mankind, and

to reaffirm faith in fundamental human rights, in the dignity and worth of the human person, in the equal rights of men and women and of nations large and small, and

to establish conditions under which justice and respect for the obligations arising from treaties and other sources of international law can be maintained, and

to promote social progress and better standards of life in larger freedom,

and for these ends

to practice tolerance and live together in peace with one another as good neighbors, and to unite our strength to maintain international peace and security, and

to ensure, by the acceptance of principles and the institution of methods, that armed force shall not be used, save in the common interest, and

to employ international machinery for the promotion of the economic and social advancement of all peoples,

have resolved to combine our efforts to accomplish these aims.

Accordingly, our respective Governments, through representatives assembled in the city of San Francisco, who have exhibited their full powers found to be in good and due form, have agreed to the present Charter of the United Nations and do hereby establish an international organization to be known as the United Nations.

Chapter I

Purposes and Principles

Article 1

The Purposes of the United Nations are:

1. To maintain international peace and security, and to that end: to take effective collective measures for the prevention and removal of threats to the peace, and for the suppression of acts of aggression or other breaches of the peace, and to bring about by peaceful means, and in conformity with the principles of justice and international law, adjustment or settlement of international disputes or situations which might lead to a breach of the peace;

2. To develop friendly relations among nations based on respect for the principle of equal rights and self-determination of peoples, and to take other appropriate measures to strengthen universal peace;

3. To achieve international cooperation in solving interna-

tional problems of an economic, social, cultural, or humanitarian character, and in promoting and encouraging respect for human rights and for fundamental freedoms for all without distinction as to race, sex, language, or religion; and

4. To be a center for harmonizing the actions of nations in the attainment of these common ends.

Article 2

The Organization and its Members, in pursuit of the Purposes stated in Article 1, shall act in accordance with the following Principles.

1. The Organization is based on the principle of the sovereign equality of all its Members.

2. All Members, in order to ensure to all of them the rights and benefits resulting from membership, shall fulfil in good faith the obligations assumed by them in accordance with the present Charter.

3. All Members shall settle their international disputes by peaceful means in such a manner that international peace and security, and justice, are not endangered.

4. All Members shall refrain in their international relations from the threat or use of force against the territorial integrity or political independence of any state, or in any other manner inconsistent with the Purposes of the United Nations.

5. All Members shall give the United Nations every assistance in any action it takes in accordance with the present Charter, and shall refrain from giving assistance to any state against which the United Nations is taking preventive or enforcement action.

6. The Organization shall ensure that states which are not Members of the United Nations act in accordance with these Principles so far as may be necessary for the maintenance of international peace and security.

7. Nothing contained in the present Charter shall authorize the United Nations to intervene in matters which are essentially within the domestic jurisdiction of any state or shall require the Members to submit such matters to settlement

under the present Charter; but this principle shall not prejudice the application of enforcement measures under Chapter
VII.

CHAPTER II

Membership

Article 3

The original Members of the United Nations shall be the
states which, having participated in the United Nations
Conference on International Organization at San Francisco, or
having previously signed the Declaration by United Nations
of January 1, 1942, sign the present Charter and ratify it in
accordance with Article 110.

Article 4

1. Membership in the United Nations is open to all other
peace-loving states which accept the obligations contained in
the present Charter and, in the judgment of the Organization, are able and willing to carry out these obligations.

2. The admission of any such state to membership in the
United Nations will be effected by a decision of the General
Assembly upon the recommendation of the Security Council.

Article 5

A Member of the United Nations against which preventive
or enforcement action has been taken by the Security Council
may be suspended from the exercise of the rights and privileges of membership by the General Assembly upon the
recommendation of the Security Council. The exercise of these
rights and privileges may be restored by the Security Council.

Article 6

A Member of the United Nations which has persistently
violated the Principles contained in the present Charter may

be expelled from the Organization by the General Assembly upon the recommendation of the Security Council.

CHAPTER III

Organs

Article 7

1. There are established as the principal organs of the United Nations: a General Assembly, a Security Council, an Economic and Social Council, a Trusteeship Council, an International Court of Justice, and a Secretariat.

2. Such subsidiary organs as may be found necessary may be established in accordance with the present Charter.

Article 8

The United Nations shall place no restrictions on the eligibility of men and women to participate in any capacity and under conditions of equality in its principal and subsidiary organs.

CHAPTER IV

The General Assembly

COMPOSITION

Article 9

1. The General Assembly shall consist of all the Members of the United Nations.

2. Each Member shall have not more than five representatives in the General Assembly.

FUNCTIONS AND POWERS

Artice 10

The General Assembly may discuss any questions or any matters within the scope of the present Charter or relating to the powers and functions of any organs provided for in the present Charter, and except as provided in Article 12, may make recommendations to the Members of the United Nations or to the Security Council or to both on any such questions or matters.

Article 11

1. The General Assembly may consider the general principles of cooperation in the maintenance of international peace and security, including the principles governing disarmament and the regulation of armaments, and may make recommendations with regard to such principles to the Members or to the Security Council or to both.

2. The General Assembly may discuss any questions relating to the maintenance of international peace and security brought before it by any Member of the United Nations, or by the Security Council, or by a state which is not a Member of the United Nations in accordance with Article 35, paragraph 2, and, except as provided in Article 12, may make recommendations with regard to any such questions to the state or states concerned or to the Security Council or to both. Any such question on which action is necessary shall be referred to the Security Council by the General Assembly either before or after discussion.

3. The General Assembly may call the attention of the Security Council to situations which are likely to endanger international peace and security.

4. The powers of the General Assembly set forth in this Article shall not limit the general scope of Article 10.

Article 12

1. While the Security Council is exercising in respect of any dispute or situation the functions assigned to it in the present Charter, the General Assembly shall not make any recommendation with regard to that dispute or situation unless the Security Council so requests.

2. The Secretary-General, with the consent of the Security Council, shall notify the General Assembly at each session of any matters relative to the maintenance of international peace

and security which are being dealt with by the Security Council and shall similarly notify the General Assembly, or the Members of the United Nations if the General Assembly is not in session, immediately the Security Council ceases to deal with such matters.

Article 13

1. The General Assembly shall initiate studies and make recommendations for the purpose of:

a. promoting international cooperation in the political field and encouraging the progressive development of international law and its codification;

b. promotiong international cooperation in the economic, social, cultural, educational, and health fields, and assisting in the realization of human rights and fundamental freedoms for all without distinction as to race, sex, language, or religion.

2. The further responsibilities, functions, and powers of the General Assembly with respect to matters mentioned in paragraph 1 (b) above are set forth in Chapters IX and X.

Article 14

Subject to the provisions of Article 12, the General Assembly may recommend measures for the peaceful adjustment of any situation, regardless of origin, which it deems likely to impair the general welfare or friendly relations among nations, including situations resulting from a violation of the provisions of the present Charter setting forth the Purposes and Principles of the United Nations.

Article 15

1. The General Assembly shall receive and consider annual and special reports from the Security Council; these reports shall include an account of the measures that the Security Council has decided upon or taken to maintain international peace and security.

2. The General Assembly shall receive and consider reports from the other organs of the United Nations.

Article 16

The General Assembly shall perform such functions with respect to the international trusteeship system as are assigned to it under Chapters XII and XIII, including the approval of the trusteeship agreements for areas not designated as strategic.

Article 17

1. The General Assembly shall consider and approve the budget of the Organization.
2. The expenses of the Organization shall be borne by the Members as apportioned by the General Assembly.
3. The General Assembly shall consider and approve any financial and budgetary arrangements with specialized agencies referred to in Article 57 and shall examine the administrative budgets of such specialized agencies with a view to making recommendations to the agencies concerned.

VOTING

Article 18

1. Each member of the General Assembly shall have one vote.
2. Decisions of the General Assembly on important questions shall be made by a two-thirds majority of the members present and voting. These questions shall include: recommendations with respect to the maintenance of international peace and security, the election of the non-permanent members of the Security Council, the election of the members of the Economic and Social Council, the election of members of the Trusteeship Council in accordance with paragraph 1 (c) of Article 86, the admission of new Members to the United Nations, the suspension of the rights and privileges of membership, the expulsion of Members, questions relating to the operation of the trusteeship system, and budgetary questions.
3. Decisions on other questions, including the determination of additional categories of questions to be decided by a

two-thirds majority, shall be made by a majority of the members present and voting.

Article 19

A member of the United Nations which is in arrears in the payment of its financial contributions to the Organization shall have no vote in the General Assembly if the amount of its arrears equals or exceeds the amount of the contributions due from it for the preceding two full years. The General Assembly may, nevertheless, permit such a Member to vote if it is satisfied that the failure to pay is due to conditions beyond the control of the Member.

PROCEDURE

Article 20

The General Assembly shall meet in regular annual sessions and in such special sessions as occasion may require. Special sessions shall be convoked by the Secretary-General at the request of the Security Council or of a majority of the Members of the of the United Nations.

Article 21

The General Assembly shall adopt its own rules of procedure. It shall elect its President for each session.

Article 22

The General Assembly may establish such subsidiary organs as it deems necessary for the performance of its functions.

CHAPTER V

The Security Council

COMPOSITION

Article 23

1. The Security Council shall consist of eleven Members of the United Nations. The Republic of China, France, the Union of Soviet Socialist Republics, the United Kingdom of

Great Britain and Northern Ireland, and the United States of America shall be permanent members of the Security Council. The General Assembly shall elect six other Members of the United Nations to be non-permanent members of the Security Council, due regard being specially paid, in the first instance to the contribution of Members of the United Nations to the maintenance of international peace and security and to the other purposes of the Organization, and also to equitable geographical distribution.

2. The non-permanent members of the Security Council shall be elected for a term of two years. In the first election of the non-permanent members, however, three shall be chosen for a term of one year. A retiring member shall not be eligible for immediate re-election.

3. Each member of the Security Council shall have one representative.

FUNCTIONS AND POWERS

Article 24

1. In order to ensure prompt and effective action by the United Nations, its Members confer on the Security Council primary responsibility for the maintenance of international peace and security, and agree that in carrying out its duties under this responsibility the Security Council acts on their behalf.

2. In discharging these duties the Security Council shall act in accordance with the Purposes and Principles of the United Nations. The specific powers granted to the Security Council for the discharge of these duties are laid down in Chapters VI, VII, VIII, and XII.

3. The Security Council shall submit annual and, when necessary, special reports to the General Assembly for its consideration.

Article 25

The Members of the United Nations agree to accept and carry out the decisions of the Security Council in accordance with the present Charter.

Article 26

In order to promote the establishment and maintenance of international peace and security with the least diversion for armaments the world's human and economic resources, the Security Council shall be responsible for formulating, with the assistance of the Military Staff Committee referred to in Article 47, plans to be submitted to the Members of the United Nations for the establishment of a system for the regulation of armaments.

VOTING

Article 27

1. Each member of the Security Council shall have one vote.
2. Decisions of the Security Council on procedural matters shall be made by an affirmative vote of seven members.
3. Decisions of the Security Council on all other matters shall be made by an affirmative vote of seven members including the concurring votes of the permanent members; provided that, in decisions under Chapter VI, and under paragraph 3 of Article 52, a party to a dispute shall abstain from voting.

PROCEDURE

Article 28

1. The Security Council shall be so organized as to be able to function continuously. Each member of the Security Council shall for this purpose be represented at all times at the seat of the Organization.
2. The Security Council shall hold periodic meetings at which each of its members may, if it so desires, be represented by a member of the government or by some other specially designated representative.
3. The Security Council may hold meetings at such places other than the seat of the Organization as in its judgment will best facilitate its work.

Article 29

The Security Council may establish such subsidiary organs as it deems necessary for the performance of its functions.

Article 30

The Security Council shall adopt its own rules of procedure, including the method of selecting its President.

Article 31

Any Member of the United Nations which is not a member of the Security Council may participate, without vote, in the discussion of any question brought before the Security Council whenever the latter considers that the interests of that Member are specially affected.

Article 32

Any Member of the United Nations which is not a member of the Security Council or any state which is not a Member of the United Nations, if it is a party to a dispute under consideration by the Security Council, shall be invited to participate, without vote, in the discussion relating to the dispute. The Security Council shall lay down such conditions as it deems just for the participation of a state which is not a Member of the United Nations.

Chapter VI

Pacific Settlement of Disputes

Article 33

1. The parties to any dispute, the continuance of which is likely to endanger the maintenance of international peace and security, shall, first of all, seek a solution by negotiation, enquiry, mediation, conciliation, arbitration, judicial settlement, resort to regional agencies or arrangements, or other peaceful means of their own choice.

2. The Security Council shall, when it deems necessary, call upon the parties to settle their dispute by such means.

Article 34

The Security Council may investigate any dispute, or any situation which might lead to international friction or give rise to a dispute, in order to determine whether the continuance of the dispute or situation is likely to endanger the maintenance of international peace and security.

Article 35

1. Any Member of the United Nations may bring any dispute, or any situation of the nature referred to in Article 34, to the attention of the Security Council or of the General Assembly.

2. A state which is not a Member of the United Nations may bring to the attention of the Security Council or of the General Assembly any dispute to which it is a party if it accepts in advance, for the purposes of the dispute, the obligations of pacific settlement provided in the present Charter.

3. The proceedings of the General Assembly in respect of matters brought to its attention under this Article will be subject to the provisions of Articles 11 and 12.

Article 36

1. The Security Council may, at any stage of a dispute of the nature referred to in Article 33 or of a situation of like nature, recommend appropriate procedures or methods of adjustment.

2. The Security Council should take into consideration any procedures for the settlement of the dispute which have already been adopted by the parties.

3. In making recommendations under this Article the Security Council should also take into consideration that legal disputes should as a general rule be referred by the parties to the International Court of Justice in accordance with the provisions of the Statute of the Court.

Article 37

1. Should the parties to a dispute of the nature referred to in Article 33 fail to settle it by the means indicated in that Article, they shall refer it to the Security Council.

2. If the Security Council deems that the continuance of the dispute is in fact likely to endanger the maintenance of international peace and security, it shall decide whether to take action under Article 36 or to recommend such terms of settlement as it may consider appropriate.

Article 38

Without prejudice to the provisions of Articles 33 to 37, the Security Council may, if all the parties to any dispute so request, make recommendations to the parties with a view to a pacific settlement of the dispute.

CHAPTER VII

Action With Respect to Threats to the Peace, Breaches of the Peace, and Acts of Aggression

Article 39

The Security Council shall determine the existence of any threat to the peace, breach of the peace, or act of aggression and shall make recommendations, or decide what measures shall be taken in accordance with Articles 41 and 42, to maintain or restore international peace and security.

Article 40

In order to prevent an aggravation of the situation, the Security Council may, before making the recommendations or deciding upon the measures provided for in Article 39, call upon the parties concerned to comply with such provisional measures as it deems necessary or desirable. Such provisional measures shall be without prejudice to the rights, claims, or position of the parties concerned. The Security Council shall duly take account of failure to comply with such provisional measures.

Article 41

The Security Council may decide what measures not involving the use of armed force are to be employed to give effect to its decisions, and it may call upon the Members of the United Nations to apply such measures. These may include complete or partial interruption of economic relations and of rail, sea, air, postal, telegraphic, radio, and other means of communication, and the severance of diplomatic relations.

Article 42

Should the Security Council consider that measures provided for in Article 41 would be inadequate or have proved to be inadequate, it may take such action by air, sea, or land forces as may be necessary to maintain or restore international peace and security. Such action may include demonstrations, blockade, and other operations by air, sea, or land forces of Members of the United Nations.

Article 43

1. All Members of the United Nations, in order to contribute to the maintenance of international peace and security, undertake to make available to the Security Council, on its call and in accordance with a special agreement or agreements, armed forces, assistance, and facilities, including rights of passage, necessary for the purpose of maintaining international peace and security.

2. Such agreement or agreements shall govern the numbers and types of forces, their degree of readiness and general location, and the nature of the facilities and assistance to be provided.

3. The agreement or agreements shall be negotiated as soon as possible on the initiative of the Security Council. They

shall be concluded between the Security Council and Members or between the Security Council and groups of Members and shall be subject to ratification by the signatory states in accordance with their respective constitutional processes.

Article 44

When the Security Council has decided to use force it shall, before calling upon a Member not represented on it to provide armed forces in fulfillment of the obligations assumed under Article 43, invite that Member, if the Member so desires, to participate in the decisions of the Security Council concerning the employment of contingents of that Member's armed forces.

Article 45

In order to enable the United Nations to take urgent military measures, Members shall hold immediately available national air-force contingents for combined international enforcement action. The strength and degree of readiness of these contingents and plans for their combined action shall be determined, within the limits laid down in the special agreement or agreements referred to in Article 43, by the Security Council with the assistance of the Military Staff Committee.

Article 46

Plans for the application of armed force shall be made by the Security Council with the assistance of the Military Staff Committee.

Article 47

1. There shall be established a Military Staff Committee to advise and assist the Security Council on all questions relating to the Security Council's military requirements for the maintenance of international peace and security, the employment and command of forces placed at its disposal, the regulation of armaments, and possible disarmament.

2. The Military Staff Committee shall consist of the Chiefs

of Staff of the permanent members of the Security Council or their representatives. Any Member of the United Nations not permanently represented on the Committee shall be invited by the Committee to be associated with it when the efficient discharge of the Committee's responsibilities requires the participation of that Member in its work.

3. The Military Staff Committee shall be responsible under the Security Council for the strategic direction of any armed forces placed at the disposal of the Security Council. Questions relating to the command of such forces shall be worked out subsequently.

4. The Military Staff Committee, with the authorization of the Security Council and after consultation with appropriate regional agencies, may establish regional subcommittees.

Article 48

1. The action required to carry out the decisions of the Security Council for the maintenance of international peace and security shall be taken by all the Members of the United Nations or by some of them, as the Security Council may determine.

2. Such decisions shall be carried out by the Members of the United Nations directly and through their action in the appropriate international agencies of which they are members.

Article 49

The Members of the United Nations shall join in affording mutual assistance in carrying out the measures decided upon by the Security Council.

Article 50

If preventive or enforcement measures against any state are taken by the Security Council, any other state, whether a Member of the United Nations or not, which finds itself confronted with special economic problems arising from the carrying out of those measures shall have the right to consult the Security Council with regard to a solution of those problems.

Article 51

Nothing in the present Charter shall impair the inherent right of individual or collective self-defense if an armed attack occurs against a Member of the United Nations, until the Security Council has taken the measures necessary to maintain international peace and security. Measures taken by Members in the exercise of this right of self-defense shall be immediately reported to the Security Council and shall not in any way affect the authority and responsibility of the Security Council under the present Charter to take at any time such action as it deems necessary in order to maintain or restore international peace and security.

CHAPTER VIII

Regional Arrangements

Article 52

1. Nothing in the present Charter precludes the existence of regional arrangements or agencies for dealing with such matters relating to the maintenance of international peace and security as are appropriate for regional action, provided that such arrangements or agencies and their activities are consistent with the Purposes and Principles of the United Nations.

2. The Members of the United Nations entering into such arrangements or constituting such agencies shall make every effort to achieve pacific settlement of local disputes through such regional arrangements or by such regional agencies before referring them to the Security Council.

3. The Security Council shall encourage the development of pacific settlement of local disputes through such regional arrangements or by such regional agencies either on the initiative of the states concerned or by reference from the Security Council.

4. This Article in no way impairs the application of Articles 34 and 35.

Article 53

1. The Security Council shall, where appropriate, utilize such regional arrangements or agencies for enforcement action under its authority. But no enforcement action shall be taken under regional arrangements or by regional agencies without the authorization of the Security Council, with the exception of measures against any enemy state, as defined in paragraph 2 of this Article, provided for pursuant to Article 107 or in regional arrangements directed against renewal of aggressive policy on the part of any such state, until such time as the Organization may, on request of the Governments concerned, be charged with the responsibility for preventing further aggression by such a state.

2. The term enemy state as used in paragraph 1 of this Article applies to any state which during the Second World War has been an enemy of any signatory of the present Charter.

Article 54

The Security Council shall at all times be kept fully informed of activities undertaken or in contemplation under regional arrangements or by regional agencies for the maintenance of international peace and security.

CHAPTER IX

International Economic and Social Cooperation

Article 55

With a view to the creation of conditions of stability and well-being which are necessary for peaceful and friendly relations among nations based on respect for the principle of equal rights and self-determination of peoples, the United Nations shall promote:

a. higher standards of living, full employment, and conditions of economic and social progress and development;

b. solutions of international economic, social, health, and related problems; and international cultural and educational cooperation; and

c. universal respect for, and observance of, human rights and fundamental freedoms for all without distinction as to race, sex, language, or religion.

Article 56

All Members pledge themselves to take joint and separate action in cooperation with the Organization for the achievement of the purposes set forth in Article 55.

Article 57

1. The various specialized agencies, established by intergovernmental agreement and having wide international responsibilities, as defined in their basic instruments, in economic, social, cultural, educational, health, and related fields, shall be brought into relationship with the United Nations in accordance with the provisions of Article 63.

2. Such agencies thus brought into relationship with the United Nations are hereinafter referred to as specialized agencies.

Article 58

The Organization shall make recommendations for the co-ordination of the policies an activities of the specialized agencies.

Article 59

The Organization shall, where appropriate, initiate negotiations among the states concerned for the creation of any new specialized agencies required for the accomplishment of the purposes set forth in Article 55.

Article 60

Responsibility for the discharge of the functions of the Organization set forth in this Chapter shall be vested in the General Assembly and, under the authority of the General Assembly, in the Economic and Social Council, which shall have for this purpose the powers set forth in Chapter X.

CHAPTER X

The Economic and Social Council

COMPOSITION

Article 61

1. The Economic and Social Council shall consist of eighteen Members of the United Nations elected by the General Assembly.

2. Subject to the provisions of paragraph 3, six members of the Economic and Social Council shall be elected each year for a term of three years. A retiring member shall be eligible for immediate re-election.

3. At the first election, eighteen members of the Economic and Social Council shall be chosen. The term of office of six members so chosen shall expire at the end of one year, and of six other members at the end of two years, in accordance with arrangements made by the General Assembly.

4. Each member of the Economic and Social Council shall have one representative.

FUNCTIONS AND POWERS

Article 62

1. The Economic and Social Council may make or initiate studies and reports with respect to international economic,

social, cultural, educational, health, and related matters and may make recommendations with respect to any such matters to the General Assembly, to the Members of the United Nations, and to the specialized agencies concerned.

2. It may make recommendations for the purpose of promoting respect for, and observance of, human rights and fundamental freedoms for all.

3. It may prepare draft conventions for submission to the General Assembly, with respect to matters falling within its competence.

4. It may call, in accordance with the rules prescribed by the United Nations, international conferences on matters falling within its competence.

Article 63

1. The Economic and Social Council may enter into agreements with any of the agencies referred to in Article 57, defining the terms on which the agency concerned shall be brought into relationship with the United Nations. Such agreements shall be subject to approval by the General Assembly.

2. It may coordinate the activities of the specialized agencies through consultation with and recommendations to such agencies and through recommendations to the General Assembly and to the Members of the United Nations.

Article 64

1. The Economic and Social Council may take appropriate steps to obtain regular reports from the specialized agencies. It may make arrangements with the Members of the United Nations and with the specialized agencies to obtain reports on the steps taken to give effect to its own recommendations and to recommendations on matters falling within its competence made by the General Assembly.

2. It may communicate its observations on these reports to the General Assembly.

Article 65

The Economic and Social Council may furnish information to the Security Council and shall assist the Security Council upon its request.

Article 66

1. The Economic and Social Council shall perform such functions as fall within its competence in connection with the carrying out of the recommendations of the General Assembly.

2. It may, with the approval of the General Assembly, perform services at the request of Members of the United Nations and at the request of specialized agencies.

3. It shall perform such other functions as are specified elsewhere in the present Charter or as may be assigned to it by the General Assembly.

VOTING

Article 67

1. Each member of the Economic and Social Council shall have one vote.

2. Decisions of the Economic and Social Council shall be made by a majority of the members present and voting.

PROCEDURE

Article 68

The Economic and Social Council shall set up commissions in economic and social fields and for the promotion of human rights, and such other commissions as may be required for the performance of its functions.

Article 69

The Economic and Social Council shall invite any Member of the United Nations to participate, without vote, in its deliberations on any matter of particular concern to that Member.

Article 70

The Economic and Social Council may make arrangements for representatives of the specialized agencies to participate, without vote, in its deliberations and in those of the commissions established by it, and for its representatives to participate in the deliberations of the specialized agencies.

Article 71

The Economic and Social Council may make suitable arrangements for consultation with non-governmental organizations which are concerned with matters within its competence. Such arrangements may be made with international organizations and, where appropriate, with national organizations after consultation with the Member of the United Nations concerned.

Article 72

1. The Economic and Social Council shall adopt its own rules of procedure, including the method of selecting its President.

2. The Economic and Social Council shall meet as required in accordance with its rules, which shall include provision for the convening of meetings on the request of a majority of its members.

Chapter XI

Declaration Regarding Non-Self-Governing Territories

Article 73

Members of the United Nations which have or assume responsibilities for the administration of territories whose peoples have not yet attained a full measure of self-government recognize the principle that the interests of the inhabitants of these territories are paramount, and accept as a sacred trust the obligation to promote to the utmost, within the system of international peace and security established by the present Charter, the well-being of the inhabitants of these territories, and, to this end:

a. to ensure, with due respect for the culture of the peoples concerned, their political, economic, social, and educational advancement, their just treatment, and their protection against abuses;

b. to develop self-government, to take due account of the political aspirations of the peoples, and to assist them in the progressive development of their free political institutions, according to the particular circumstances of each territory and its peoples and their varying stages of advancement;

c. to further international peace and security;

d. to promote constructive measures of development, to encourage research, and to cooperate with one another and, when and where appropriate, with specialized international bodies with a view to the practical achievement of the social, economic, and scientific purposes set forth in this Article and

e. to transmit regularly to the Secretary-General for information purposes, subject to such limitation as security and constitutional considerations may require, statistical and other information of a technical nature relating to economic, social, and educational conditions in the territories for which they are respectively responsible other than those territories to which Chapters XII and XIII apply.

Article 74

Members of the United Nations also agree that their policy in respect of the territories to which this Chapter applies, no less than in respect of their metropolitan areas, must be based on the general principle of good-neighborliness, due account being taken of the interests and well-being of the rest of the world, in social, economic, and commercial matters.

CHAPTER XII
International Trusteeship System
Article 75

The United Nations shall establish under its authority an international trusteeship system for the administration and supervision of such territories as may be placed thereunder by subsequent individual agreements. These territories are hereinafter referred to as trust territories.

Article 76

The basic objectives of the trusteeship system, in accordance with the Purposes of the United Nations laid down in Article 1 of the present Charter, shall be:

a. to further international peace and security

b. to promote the political, economic, social, and educational advancement of the inhabitants of the trust territories, and their progressive development towards self-government or independence as may be appropriate to the particular circumstances of each territory and its peoples and the freely expressed wishes of the peoples concerned, and as may be provided by the terms of each trusteeship agreement;

c. to encourage respect for human rights and for fundamental freedoms for all without distinction as to race, sex, language, or religion, and to encourage recognition of the interdependence of the peoples of the world; and

d. to ensure equal treatment in social, economic, and commercial matters for all Members of the United Nations and their nationals, and also equal treatment for the latter in the administration of justice, without prejudice to the attainment of the foregoing objectives and subject to the provisions of Article 80.

Article 77

1. The trusteeship system shall apply to such territories in the following categories as may be placed thereunder by means of trusteeship agreements:

a. territories now held under mandate;

b. territories which may be detached from enemy states as a result of the Second World War; and

c. territories voluntarily placed under the system by states responsible for their administration.

2. It will be a matter for subsequent agreement as to which territories in the foregoing categories will be brought under the trusteeship system and upon what terms.

Article 78

The trusteeship system shall not apply to territories which have become Members of the United Nations, relationship among which shall be based on respect for the principle of sovereign equality.

Article 79

The terms of trusteeship for each territory to be placed under the trusteeship system, including any alteration or amendment, shall be agreed upon by the states directly concerned, including the mandatory power in the case of territories held under mandate by a Member of the United Nations, and shall be approved as provided for in Articles 83 and 85.

Article 80

1. Except as may be agreed upon in individual trusteeship agreements, made under Articles 77, 79, and 81, placing each territory under the trusteeship system, and until such agreements have been concluded, nothing in this Chapter shall be construed in or of itself to alter in any manner the rights whatsoever of any states or any peoples or the terms of existing international instruments to which Members of the United Nations may respectively be parties.

2. Paragraph 1 of this Article shall not be interpreted as giving grounds for delay or postponement of the negotiation and conclusion of agreements for placing mandated and other territories under the trusteeship system as provided for in Article 77.

Article 81

The trusteeship agreement shall in each case include the terms under which the trust territory will be administered and designate the authority which will exercise the administration of the trust territory. Such authority, hereinafter called the administering authority, may be one or more states or the Organization itself.

Article 82

There may be designated, in any trusteeship agreement, a strategic area or areas which may include part or all of the trust territory to which the agreement applies, without prejudice to any special agreement or agreements made under Article 43.

Article 83

1. All functions of the United Nations relating to strategic areas, including the approval of the terms of the trusteeship agreements and of their alteration or amendment, shall be exercised by the Security Council.

2. The basic objectives set forth in Article 76 shall be applicable to the people of each strategic area.

3. The Security Council shall, subject to the provisions of the trusteeship agreements and without prejudice to security considerations, avail itself of the assistance of the Trusteeship Council to perform those functions of the United Nations under the trusteeship system relating to political, economic, social, and educational matters in the strategic areas.

Article 84

It shall be the duty of the administering authority to ensure that the trust territory shall play its part in the maintenance of international peace and security. To this end the administering authority may make use of volunteer forces, facilities, and assistance from the trust territory in carrying out the obligations towards the Security Council undertaken in this regard by the administering authority, as well as for local defense and the maintenance of law and order within the trust territory.

Article 85

1. The functions of the United Nations with regard to trusteeship agreements for all areas not designated as strategic, including the approval of the terms of the trusteeship agreements and of their alteration or amendment, shall be exercised by the General Assembly.

2. The Trusteeship Council, operating under the authority of the General Assembly, shall assist the General Assembly in carrying out these functions.

CHAPTER XIII

The Trusteeship Council

COMPOSITION

Article 86

1. The Trusteeship Council shall consist of the following Members of the United Nations:

a. those Members administering trust territories;

b. such of those Members mentioned by name in Article 23 as are not administering trust territories; and

c. as many other Members elected for three-year terms by the General Assembly as may be necessary to ensure that the total number of members of the Trusteeship Council is equally divided between those Members of the United Nations which administer trust territories and those which do not.

2. Each member of the Trusteeship Council shall designate one specially qualified person to represent it therein.

FUNCTIONS AND POWERS

Article 87

The General Assembly and, under its authority, the Trusteeship Council, in carrying out their functions, may:

a. consider reports submitted by the administering authority;

b. accept petitions and examine them in consultation with the administering authority;

c. provide for periodic visits to the respective trust territories at times agreed upon with the administering authority; and

d. take these and other actions in conformity with the terms of the trusteeship agreements.

Article 88

The Trusteeship Council shall formulate a questionnaire on the political, economic, social, and educational advancement of the inhabitants of each trust territory, and the administering authority for each trust territory within the competence of the General Assembly shall make an annual report to the General Assembly upon the basis of such questionnaire.

VOTING

Article 89

1. Each member of the Trusteeship Council shall have one vote.

2. Decisions of the Trusteeship Council shall be made by a majority of the members present and voting.

PROCEDURE

Article 90

1. The Trusteeship Council shall adopt its own rules of procedure, including the method of selecting its President,

2. The Trusteeship Council shall meet as required in accordance with its rules, which shall include provision for the convening of meetings on the request of a majority of its members.

Article 91

The Trusteeship Council shall, when appropriate, avail itself of the assistance of the Economic and Social Council and of the Specialized agencies in regard to matters with which they are respectively concerned.

CHAPTER XIV

The International Court of Justice

Article 92

The International Court of Justice shall be the principal judicial organ of the United Nations. It shall function in accordance with the annexed Statute, which is based upon the Statute of the Permanent Court of International Justice and forms an integral part of the present Charter.

Article 93

1. All Members of the United Nations are *ipso facto* parties to the Statute of the International Court of Justice.

2. A state which is not a Member of the United Nations may become a party to the Statute of the International Court of Justice on conditions to be determined in each case by the General Assembly upon the recommendation of the Security Council.

Article 94

1. Each Member of the United Nations undertakes to comply with the decision of the International Court of Justice in any case to which it is a party.

2. If any party to a case fails to perform the obligations incumbent upon it under a judgment rendered by the Court, the other party may have recourse to the Security Council, which may, if it deems necessary, make recommendations or decide upon measures to be taken to give effect to the judgment.

Article 95

Nothing in the present Charter shall prevent Members of the United Nations from entrusting the solution of their differences to other tribunals by virtue of agreements already in existence or which may be concluded in the future.

Article 96

1. The General Assembly or the Security Council may request the International Court of Justice to give an advisory opinion on any legal question.

2. Other organs of the United Nations and specialized agencies, which may at any time be so authorized by the General Assembly, may also request advisory opinions of the Court on legal questions arising within the scope of their activities.

CHAPTER XV

The Secretariat

Article 97

The Secretariat shall comprise a Secretary-General and such staff as the Organization may require. The Secretary-General shall be appointed by the General Assembly upon the recommendation of the Security Council. He shall be the chief administrative officer of the Organization.

Article 98

The Secretary-General shall act in that capacity in all meetings of the General Assembly, of the Security Council, of the Economic and Social Council, and of the Trusteeship Council, and shall perform such other functions as are entrusted to him by these organs. The Secretary-General shall make an annual report to the General Assembly on the work of the Organization.

Article 99

The Secretary-General may bring to the attention of the Security Council any matter which in his opinion may threaten the maintenance of international peace and security.

Article 100

1. In the performance of their duties the Secretary-General and the staff shall not seek or receive instructions from any government or from any other authority external to the Organization. They shall refrain from any action which might reflect on their position as international officials responsible only to the Organization.

2. Each Member of the United Nations undertakes to respect the exclusively international character of the responsibilities of the Secretary-General and the staff and not to seek to influence them in the discharge of their responsibilities.

Article 101

1. The staff shall be appointed by the Secretary-General under regulations established by the General Assembly.

2. Appropriate staffs shall be permanently assigned to the Economic and Social Council, the Trusteeship Council, and, as required, to other organs of the United Nations. These staffs shall form a part of the Secretariat.

3. The paramount consideration in the employment of the staff and in the determination of the conditions of service shall be the necessity of securing the highest standards of efficiency, competence, and integrity. Due regard shall be paid to the importance of recruiting the staff on as wide a geographical basis as possible.

CHAPTER XVI

Miscellaneous Provisions

Article 102

1. Every treaty and every international agreement entered into by any Member of the United Nations after the present Charter comes into force shall as soon as possible be registered with the Secretariat and published by it.

2. No party to any such treaty or international agreement which has not been registered in accordance with the provi-

sions of paragraph 1 of this Article may invoke that treaty or agreement before any organ of the United Nations.

Article 103

In the event of a conflict between the obligations of the Members of the United Nations under the present Charter and their obligations under any other international agreement, their obligations under the present Charter shall prevail.

Article 104

The Organization shall enjoy in the territory of each of its Members such legal capacity as may be necessary for the exercise of its functions and the fulfillment of its purposes.

Article 105

1. The Organization shall enjoy in the territory of each of its Members such privileges and immunities as are necessary for the fulfillment of its purposes.

2. Representatives of the Members of the United Nations and officials of the Organization shall similarly enjoy such privileges and immunities as are necessary for the independent exercise of their functions in connection with the Organization.

3. The General Assembly may make recommendations with a view to determining the details of the application of paragraphs 1 and 2 of this Article or may propose conventions to the Members of the United Nations for this purpose.

CHAPTER XVII

Transitional Security Arrangements

Article 106

Pending the coming into force of such special agreements referred to in Article 43 as in the opinion of the Security Council enable it to begin the exercise of its responsibilities under Article 42, the parties to the Four-Nation Declaration, signed at Moscow, October 30, 1943, and France, shall, in accordance with the provisions of paragraph 5 of that Declaration, consult with one another and as occasion requires with other Members of the United Nations with a view to such joint action on behalf of the Organization as may be necessary for the purpose of maintaining international peace and security.

Article 107

Nothing in the present Charter shall invalidate or preclude action, in relation to any state which during the Second World War has been an enemy of any signatory to the present Charter, taken or authorized as a result of that war by the Governments having responsibility for such action.

CHAPTER XVIII

Amendments

Article 108

Amendments to the present Charter shall come into force for all Members of the United Nations when they have been adapted by a vote of two thirds of the members of the General Assembly and ratified in accordance with their respective constitutional processes by two thirds of the Members of the United Nations, including all the permanent members of the Security Council.

Article 109

1. A General Conference of the Members of the United Nations for the purpose of reviewing the present Charter may be held at a date and place to be fixed by a two-thirds vote of the members of the General Assembly and by a vote of any seven members of the Security Council. Each Member of the United Nations shall have one vote in the conference.

2. Any alteration of the present Charter recommended by a

two-thirds vote of the conference shall take effect when ratified in accordance with their respective constitutional processes by two thirds of the Members of the United Nations including all the permanent members of the Security Council.

3. If such a conference has not been held before the tenth annual session of the General Assembly following the coming into force of the present Charter, the proposal to call such a conference shall be placed on the agenda of that session of the General Assembly, and the conference shall be held if so decided by a majority vote of the members of the General Assembly and by a vote of any seven members of the Security Council.

Chapter XIX

Ratification and Signature

Article 110

1. The present Charter shall be ratified by the signatory states in accordance with their respective constitutional processes.

2. The ratifications shall be deposited with the Government of the United States of America, which shall notify all the signatory states of each deposit as well as the Secretary-General of the Organization when he has been appointed.

3. The present Charter shall come into force upon the deposit of ratifications by the Republic of China, France, the Union of Soviet Socialist Republics, the United Kingdom of Great Britain and Northern Ireland, and the United States of America, and by a majority of the other signatory states. A protocol of the ratifications deposited shall thereupon be drawn up by the Government of the United States of America which shall communicate copies thereof to all the signatory states.

4. The states signatory to the present Charter which ratify it after it has come into force will become original Members of

the United Nations on the date of the deposit of their respective ratifications.

Article 111

The present Charter, of which the Chinese, French, Russian, English, and Spanish texts are equally authentic, shall remain deposited in the archives of the Government of the United States of America. Duly certified copies thereof shall be transmitted by that Government to the Governments of the other signatory states.

IN FAITH WHEREOF the representatives of the Governments of the United Nations have signed the present Charter.

DONE at the city of San Francisco the twenty-sixth day of June, one thousand nine hundred and forty-five.

The following countries are signatory to the Charter:

CHINA

UNION OF SOVIET SOCIALIST REPUBLICS

UNITED KINGDOM OF GREAT BRITAIN AND NORTHERN IRELAND

UNITED STATES OF AMERICA

FRANCE

ARGENTINA

AUSTRALIA

BELGIUM

BOLIVIA

BRAZIL

BYELORUSSIAN SOVIET SOCIALIST REPUBLIC

CANADA

CHILI

COLOMBIA

COSTA RICA

CUBA

CZECHOSLOVAKIA

DENMARK

DOMINICAN REPUBLIC

ECUADOR

EGYPT

EL SALVADOR

ETHIOPIA

GREECE

GUATEMALA

HAITI

HONDURAS

INDIA

IRAN

IRAQ

LEBANON

LIBERIA

LUXEMBOURG

MEXICO

NETHERLANDS

NEW ZEALAND

NICARAGUA

NORWAY

PANAMA

PARAGUAY

PERU

PHILIPPINE COMMONWEALTH

POLAND

SAUDI ARABIA

SYRIA

TURKEY

UKRAINIAN SOVIET SOCIALIST REPUBLIC

UNION OF SOUTH AFRICA

URUGUAY

VENEZUELA

YUGOSLAVIA

Appendix B:
Statute of the International Court of Justice

Article 1

The international court of justice established by the Charter of the United Nations as the principal judicial organ of the United Nations shall be constituted and shall function in accordance with the provisions of the present Statute.

CHAPTER I

Organization of the Court

Article 2

The Court shall be composed of a body of independent judges, elected regardless of their nationality from among persons of high moral character, who possess the qualifications required in their respective countries for appointment to the highest judicial offices, or are juris-consults of recognized competence in international law.

Article 3

1. The Court shall consist of fifteen members, no two of whom may be nationals of the same state.

2. A person who for the purposes of membership in the Court could be regarded as a national of more than one state shall be deemed to be a national of the one in which he ordinarily exercises civil and political rights.

Article 4

1. The members of the Court shall be elected by the General Assembly and by the Security Council from a list of persons nominated by the national groups in the Permanent Court of Arbitration, in accordance with the following provisions.

2. In the case of Members of the United Nations not represented in the Permanent Court of Arbitration, candidates shall be nominated by national groups appointed for this purpose by their governments under the same conditions as those prescribed for members of the Permanent Court of Arbitration by Article 44 of the Convention of The Hague of 1907 for the pacific settlement of international disputes.

3. The conditions under which a state which is a party to the present Statute but is not a Member of the United Nations may participate in electing the members of the Court shall, in the absence of a special agreement, be laid down by the General Assembly upon recommendation of the Security Council.

Article 5

1. At least three months before the date of the election, the Secretary-General of the United Nations shall address a written request to the members of the Permanent Court of Arbitration belonging to the states which are parties to the present Statute, and to the members of the national groups appointed under Article 4, paragraph 2, inviting them to undertake, within a given time, by national groups, the nomination of persons in a position to accept the duties of a member of the Court.

2. No group may nominate more than four persons, not more than two of whom shall be of their own nationality. In no case may the number of candidates nominated by a group be more than double the number of seats to be filled.

Article 6

Before making these nominations, each national group is recommended to consult its highest court of justice, its legal faculties and schools of law, and its national academies and national sections of international academies devoted to the study of law.

Article 7

1. The Secretary-General shall prepare a list in alphabetical order of all the persons thus nominated. Save as provided in Article 12, paragraph 2, these shall be the only persons eligible.
2. The Secretary-General shall submit this list to the General Assembly and to the Security Council.

Article 8

The General Assembly and the Security Council shall proceed independently of one another to elect the members of the Court.

Article 9

At every election, the electors shall bear in mind not only that the persons to be elected should individually possess the qualifications required, but also that in the body as a whole the representation of the main forms of civilization and of the principal legal systems of the world should be assured.

Article 10

1. Those candidates who obtain an absolute majority of votes in the General Assembly and in the Security Council shall be considered as elected.
2. Any vote of the Security Council, whether for the election of judges or for the appointment of members of the conference envisaged in Article 12, shall be taken without any

distinction between permanent and non-permanent members of the Security Council.

3. In the event of more than one national of the same state obtaining an absolute majority of the votes both of the General Assembly and of the Security Council, the eldest of these only shall be considered as elected.

Article 11

If, after the first meeting held for the purpose of the election, one or more seats remain to be filled, a second and, if necessary, a third meeting shall take place.

Article 12

1. If, after the third meeting, one or more seats still remain unfilled, a joint conference consisting of six members, three appointed by the General Assembly and three by the Security Council, may be formed at any time at the request of either the General Assembly or the Security Council, for the purpose of choosing by the vote of an absolute majority one name for each seat still vacant, to submit to the General Assembly and the Security Council for their respective acceptance.

2. If the joint conference is unanimously agreed upon any person who fulfils the required conditions, he may be included in its list, even though he was not included in the list of nominations referred to in Article 7.

3. If the joint conference is satisfied that it will not be successful in procuring an election, those members of the Court who have already been elected shall, within a period to be fixed by the Security Council, proceed to fill the vacant seats by selection from among those candidates who have obtained votes either in the General Assembly or in the Security Council.

4. In the event of an equality of votes among the judges, the eldest judge shall have a casting vote.

Article 13

1. The members of the Court shall be elected for nine years and may be re-elected; provided, however, that the judges

elected at the first election, the terms of five judges shall expire at the end of three years and the terms of five more judges shall expire at the end of six years.

2. The judges whose terms are to expire at the end of the above-mentioned initial periods of three and six years shall be chosen by lot to be drawn by the Secretary-General immediately after the first election has been completed.

3. The members of the Court shall continue to discharge their duties until their places have been filled. Though replaced, they shall finish any cases which they may have begun.

4. In the case of the resignation of a member of the Court, the resignation shall be addressed to the President of the Court for transmission to the Secretary-General. This last notification makes the place vacant.

Article 14

Vacancies shall be filled by the same method as that laid down for the first election, subject to the following provision: the Secretary-General shall, within one month of the occurrence of the vacancy, proceed to issue the invitations provided for in Article 5, and the date of the election shall be fixed by the Security Council.

Article 15

A member of the Court elected to replace a member whose term of office has not expired shall hold office for the remainder of his predecessor's term.

Article 16

1. No member of the Court may exercise any political or administrative function, or engage in any other occupation of a professional nature.

2. Any doubt on this point shall be settled by the decision of the Court.

Article 17

1. No member of the Court may act as agent, counsel, or advocate in any case.

2. No member may participate in the decision of any case in which he has previously taken part as agent, counsel, or advocate for one of the parties, or as a member of a national or international court, or of a commission of enquiry, or in any other capacity.

3. Any doubt on this point shall be settled by the decision of the Court.

Article 18

1. No member of the Court can be dismissed unless, in the unanimous opinion of the other members, he has ceased to fulfil the required conditions.

2. Formal notification thereof shall be made to the Secretary-General by the Registrar.

3. This notification makes the place vacant.

Article 19

The members of the Court, when engaged on the business of the Court, shall enjoy diplomatic privileges and immunities.

Article 20

Every member of the Court shall, before taking up his duties, make a solemn declaration in open court that he will exercise his powers impartially and conscientiously.

Article 21

1. The Court shall elect its President and Vice-President for three years; they may be re-elected.

2. The Court shall appoint its Registrar and may provide for the appointment of such other officers as may be necessary.

Article 22

1. The seat of the Court shall be established at The Hague. This, however, shall not prevent the Court from sitting and exercising its functions elsewhere whenever the Court considers it desirable.

2. The President and the Registrar shall reside at the seat of the Court.

Article 23

1. The Court shall remain permanently in session, except during the judicial vacations, the dates and duration of which shall be fixed by the Court.

2. Members of the Court are entitled to periodic leave, the dates and duration of which shall be fixed by the Court, having in mind the distance between The Hague and the home of each judge.

3. Members of the Court shall be bound, unless they are on leave or prevented from attending by illness or other serious reasons duly explained to the President, to hold themselves permanently at the disposal of the Court.

Article 24

1. If, for some special reason, a member of the Court considers that he should not take part in the decision of a particular case, he shall so inform the President.

2. If the President considers that for some special reason one of the members of the Court should not sit in a particular case, he shall give him notice accordingly.

3. If in any such case the member of the Court and the President disagree, the matter shall be settled by the decision of the Court.

Article 25

1. The full Court shall sit except when it is expressly provided otherwise in the present Statute.

2. Subject to the condition that the number of judges available to constitute the Court is not thereby reduced below eleven, the Rules of the Court may provide for allowing one or more judges, according to circumstances and in rotation, to be dispensed from sitting.

3. A quorum of nine judges shall suffice to constitute the Court.

Article 26

1. The Court may from time to time form one or more chambers, composed of three or more judges as the Court may determine, for dealing with particular categories of cases; for example, labor cases and cases relating to transit and communications.

2. The Court may at any time form a chamber for dealing with a particular case. The number of judges to constitute such a chamber shall be determined by the Court with the approval of the parties.

3. Cases shall be heard and determined by the chambers provided for in this Article if the parties so request.

Article 27

A judgment given by any of the chambers provided for in Articles 26 and 29 shall be considered as rendered by the Court.

Article 28

The chambers provided for in Articles 26 and 29 may, with the consent of the parties, sit and exercise their functions elsewhere than at The Hague.

Article 29

With a view to the speedy despatch of business, the Court shall form annually a chamber composed of five judges which, at the request of the parties, may hear and determine cases by summary procedure. In addition, two judges shall be selected for the purpose of replacing judges who find it impossible to sit.

Article 30

1. The Court shall frame rules for carrying out its functions. In particular, it shall lay down rules of procedure.

2. The Rules of the Court may provide for assessors to sit

with the Court or with any of its chambers, without the right to vote.

Article 31

1. Judges of the nationality of each of the parties shall retain their right to sit in the case before the Court.

2. If the Court includes upon the Bench a judge of the nationality of one of the parties, any other party may choose a person to sit as judge. Such person shall be chosen preferably from among those persons who have been nominated as candidates as provided in Articles 4 and 5.

3. If the Court includes upon the Bench no judge of the nationality of the parties, each of these parties may proceed to choose a judge as provided in paragraph 2 of this Article.

4. The provisions of this Article shall apply to the case of Articles 26 and 29. In such cases, the President shall request one or, if necessary, two of the members of the Court forming the chamber to give place to the members of the Court of the nationality of the parties concerned, and, failing such, or if they are unable to be present, to the judges specially chosen by the parties.

5. Should there be several parties in the same interest, they shall, for the purpose of the preceding provisions, be reckoned as one party only. Any doubt upon this point shall be settled by the decision of the Court.

6. Judges chosen as laid down in paragraphs 2, 3, and 4 of this Article shall fulfil the conditions required by Articles 2, 17 (paragraph 2), 20, and 24 of the present Statute. They shall take part in the decision on terms of complete equality with their colleagues.

Article 32

1. Each member of the Court shall receive an annual salary.

2. The President shall receive a special annual allowance.

3. The Vice-President shall receive a special allowance for every day on which he acts as President.

4. The judges chosen under Article 31, other than members

of the Court, shall receive compensation for each day on which they exercise their functions.

5. These salaries, allowances, and compensation shall be fixed by the General Assembly. They may not be decreased during the term of office.

6. The salary of the Registrar shall be fixed by the General Assembly on the proposal of the Court.

7. Regulations made by the General Assembly shall fix the conditions under which retirement pensions may be given to members of the Court and to the Registrar, and the conditions under which members of the Court and the Registrar shall have their traveling expenses refunded.

8. The above salaries, allowances, and compensation shall be free of all taxation.

Article 33

The expenses of the Court shall be borne by the United Nations in such a manner as shall be decided by the General Assembly.

CHAPTER II

Competence of the Court

Article 34

1. Only states may be parties in cases before the Court.

2. The Court, subject to and in conformity with its Rules, may request of public international organizations information relevant to cases before it, and shall receive such information presented by such organizations on their own initiative.

3. Whenever the construction of the constituent instrument of a public international organization or of an international convention adopted thereunder is in question in a case before the Court, the Registrar shall so notify the public international organization concerned and shall communicate to it copies of all the written proceedings.

Article 35

1. The Court shall be open to the states parties to the present Statute.

2. The conditions under which the Court shall be open to other states shall, subject to the special provisions contained in treaties in force, be laid down by the Security Council, but in no case shall such conditions place the parties in a position of inequality before the Court.

3. When a state which is not a Member of the United Nations is a party to a case, the Court shall fix the amount which that party is to contribute towards the expenses of the Court. This provision shall not apply if such state is bearing a share of the expenses of the Court.

Article 36

1. The jurisdiction of the Court comprises all cases which the parties refer to it and all matters specially provided for in the Charter of the United Nations or in treaties and conventions in force.

2. The states parties to the present Statute may at any time declare that they recognize as compulsory *ipso facto* and without special agreement, in relation to any other state accepting the same obligation, the jurisdiction of the Court in all legal disputes concerning:

a. the interpretation of a treaty;

b. any question of international law;

c. the existence of any fact which, if established, would constitute a breach of an international obligation;

d. the nature or extent of the reparation to be made for the breach of an international obligation.

3. The declarations referred to above may be made unconditionally or on condition of reciprocity on the part of several or certain states, or for a certain time.

4. Such declarations shall be deposited with the Secretary-General of the United Nations, who shall transmit copies

thereof to the parties to the Statute and to the Registrar of the Court.

5. Declarations made under Article 36 of the Statute of the Permanent Court of International Justice and which are still in force shall be deemed, as between the parties to the present Statute, to be acceptances of the compulsory jurisdiction of the International Court of Justice for the period which they still have to run and in accordance with their terms.

6. In the event of a dispute as to whether the Court has jurisdiction, the matter shall be settled by the decision of the Court.

Article 37

Whenever a treaty or convention in force provides for reference of a matter to a tribunal to have been instituted by the League of Nations, or to the Permanent Court of International Justice, the matter shall, as between the parties to the present Statute, be referred to the International Court of Justice.

Article 38

1. The Court, whose function is to decide in accordance with international law such disputes as are submitted to it, shall apply:

a. international conventions, whether general or particular, establishing rules expressly recognized by the contesting states;

b. international custom, as evidence of a general practice accepted as law;

c. the general principles of law recognized by civilized nations;

d. subject to the provisions of Article 59, judicial decisions and the teachings of the most highly qualified publicists of the various nations, as subsidiary means for the determination of rules of law.

2. This provision shall not prejudice the power of the Court to decide a case *ex aequo et bono,* if the parties agree thereto.

CHAPTER III
Procedure

Article 39

1. The official languages of the Court shall be French and English. If the parties agree that the case shall be conducted in French, the judgment shall be delivered in French. If the parties agree that the case shall be conducted in English, the judgment shall be delivered in English.

2. In the absence of an agreement as to which language shall be employed, each party may, in the pleadings, use the language which it prefers; the decision of the Court shall be given in French and English. In this case the Court shall at the same time determine which of the two texts shall be considered as authoritative.

3. The Court shall, at the request of any party, authorize a language other than French or English to be used by that party.

Article 40

1. Cases are brought before the the Court, as the case may be, either by the notification of the special agreement or by a written application addressed to the Registrar. In either case the subject of the dispute and the parties shall be indicated.

2. The Registrar shall forthwith communicate the application to all concerned.

3. He shall also notify the Members of the United Nations through the Secretary-General, and also any other states entitled to appear before the Court.

Article 41

1. The Court shall have the power to indicate, if it considers that circumstances so require, any provisional measures which

ought to be taken to preserve the respective rights of either party.

2. Pending the final decision, notice of the measures suggested shall forthwith be given to the parties and to the Security Council.

Article 42

1. The parties shall be represented by agents.

2. They may have the assistance of counsel or advocates before the Court.

3. The agents, counsel, and advocates of parties before the Court shall enjoy the privileges and immunities necessary to the independent exercise of their duties.

Article 43

1. The procedure shall consist of two parts: written and oral.

2. The written proceedings shall consist of the communication to the Court and to the parties of memorials, counter-memorials and, if necessary, replies; also all papers and documents in support.

3. These communications shall be made through the Registrar, in the order and within the time fixed by the Court.

4. A certified copy of every document produced by one party shall be communicated to the other party.

5. The oral proceedings shall consist of the hearing by the Court of witnesses, experts, agents, counsel, and advocates.

Article 44

1. For the service of all notices upon persons other than the agents, counsel, and advocates, the Court shall apply direct to the government of the state upon whose territory the notice has to be served.

2. The same provision shall apply whenever steps are to be taken to procure evidence on the spot.

Article 45

The hearing shall be under the control of the President or, if he is unable to preside, of the Vice-President; if neither is able to preside, the senior judge present shall preside.

Article 46

The hearing in Court shall be public, unless the Court shall decide otherwise, or unless the parties demand that the public be not admitted.

Article 47

1. Minutes shall be made at each hearing and signed by the Registrar and the President.
2. These minutes alone shall be authentic.

Article 48

The Court shall make orders for the conduct of the case, shall decide the form and time in which each party must conclude its arguments, and make all arrangements connected with the taking of evidence.

Article 49

The Court may, even before the hearing begins, call upon the agents to produce any document or to supply any explanations. Formal note shall be taken of any refusal.

Article 50

The Court may, at any time, entrust any individual, body, bureau, commission, or other organization that it may select, with the task of carrying out an enquiry or giving an expert opinion.

Article 51

During the hearing any relevant questions are to be put to the witnesses and experts under the conditions laid down by

the Court in the rules of procedure referred to in Article
30.

Article 52

After the Court has received the proofs and evidence within
the time specified for the purpose, it may refuse to accept any
further oral or written evidence that one party may desire to
present unless the other side consents.

Article 53

1. Whenever one of the parties does not appear before the
Court, or fails to defend its case, the other party may call upon
the Court to decide in favor of its claim.

2. The Court must, before doing so, satisfy itself, not only
that it has jurisdiction in accordance with Articles 36 and 37,
but also that the claim is well founded in fact and law.

Article 54

1. When, subject to the control of the Court, the agents,
counsel, and advocates have completed their presentation of
the case, the President shall declare the hearing closed.

2. The Court shall withdraw to consider the judgment.

3. The deliberations of the Court shall take place in private
and remain secret.

Article 55

1. All questions shall be decided by a majority of the judges
present.

2. In the event of an equality of votes, the President or the
judge who acts in his place shall have a casting vote.

Article 56

1. The judgment shall state the reasons on which it is
based.

2. It shall contain the names of the judges who have taken
part in the decision.

Article 57

If the judgment does not represent in whole or in part the unanimous opinion of the judges, any judge shall be entitled to deliver a separate opinion.

Article 58

The judgment shall be signed by the President and by the Registrar. It shall be read in open court, due notice having been given to the agents.

Article 59

The decision of the Court has no binding force except between the parties and in respect of that particular case.

Article 60

The judgment is final and without appeal. In the event of dispute as to the meaning or scope of the judgment, the Court shall construe it upon the request of any party.

Article 61

1. An application for revision of a judgment may be made only when it is based upon the discovery of some fact of such a nature as to be a decisive factor, which fact was, when the judgment was given, unknown to the Court and also to the party claiming revision, always provided that such ignorance was not due to negligence.

2. The proceedings for revision shall be opened by a judgment of the Court expressly recording the existence of the new fact, recognizing that it has such a character as to lay the case open to revision, and declaring the application admissible on this ground.

3. The Court may require previous compliance with the terms of the judgment before it admits proceedings in revision.

4. The application for revision must be made at latest within six months of the discovery of the new fact.

5. No application for revision may be made after the lapse of ten years from the date of the judgment.

Article 62

1. Should a state consider that it has an interest of a legal nature which may be affected by the decision in the case, it may submit a request to the Court to be permitted to intervene.

2. It shall be for the Court to decide upon this request.

Article 63

1. Whenever the construction of a convention to which states other than those concerned in the case are parties is in question, the Registrar shall notify all such states forthwith.

2. Every state so notified has the right to intervene in the proceedings; but if it uses this right, the construction given by the judgment will be equally binding upon it.

Article 64

Unless otherwise decided by the Court, each party shall bear its own costs.

Chapter IV

Advisory Opinions

Article 65

1. The Court may give an advisory opinion on any legal question at the request of whatever body may be authorized by or in accordance with the Charter of the United Nations to make such a request.

2. Questions upon which the advisory opinion of the Court is asked shall be laid before the Court by means of a written request containing an exact statement of the question upon which an opinion is required, and accompanied by all documents likely to throw light upon the question.

Article 66

1. The Registrar shall forthwith give notice of the request for an advisory opinion to all states entitled to appear before the Court.

2. The Registrar shall also, by means of a special and direct communication, notify any state entitled to appear before the Court or international organization considered by the Court, or, should it not be sitting, by the President, as likely to be able to furnish information on the question, that the Court will be prepared to receive, within a time limit to be fixed by The President, written statements, or to hear, at a public sitting to be held for the purpose, oral statements relating to the question.

3. Should any such state entitled to appear before the Court have failed to receive the special communication referred to in paragraph 2 of this Article, such state may express a desire to submit a written statement or to be heard; and the Court will decide.

4. States and organizations having presented written or oral statements or both shall be permitted to comment on the statements made by other states or organizations in the form, to the extent, and within the time limits which the Court, or, should it not be sitting, the President, shall decide in each particular case. Accordingly, the Registrar shall in due time communicate any such written statements to states and organizations having submitted similar statements.

Article 67

The Court shall deliver its advisory opinions in open court, notice having been given to the Secretary-General and to the representatives of Members of the United Nations, of other states and of international organizations immediately concerned.

Article 68

In the exercise of its advisory functions the Court shall further be guided by the provisions of the present Statute which apply in contentious cases to the extent to which it recognizes them to be applicable.

CHAPTER V

Amendment

Article 69

Amendments to the present Statute shall be effected by the same procedure as is provided by the Charter of the United Nations for amendments to that Charter, subject however to any provisions which the General Assembly upon recommendation of the Security Council may adopt concerning the participation of states which are parties to the present Statute but are not Members of the United Nations.

Article 70

The Court shall have power to propose such amendments to the present Statute as it may deem necessary, through written communications to the Secretary-General, for consideration in conformity with the provisions of Article 69.

Index